EXPLORING
THE BIBLE
WITH CHILDREN

EXPLORING THE BIBLE WITH CHILDREN

Dorothy Jean Furnish

ABINGDON   Nashville

Library of Congress Cataloging in Publication Data

FURNISH, DOROTHY JEAN, 1921-
  Exploring the Bible with children.
  Bibliography: p.
  1. Bible—Study. 2. Children—Religious life.
I. Title
BS600.2.F87   220'.07   74-34486

ISBN 0-687-12426-3

Scripture quotations are from the Revised Standard Version of the Bible, copyrighted 1946, 1952, and 1971, by the Division of Christian Education, National Council of Churches, and are used by permission.

Selected activities on pages 128, 133, 143-49 are from *Jesus,* by Mary Jo Osterman and Dorothy Jean Furnish, forthcoming.

MANUFACTURED BY THE PARTHENON PRESS AT NASHVILLE, TENNESSEE, UNITED STATES OF AMERICA

Remembering my parsonage home
where Bible meanings
were lived

ACKNOWLEDGMENTS

Although creativity is a result of individual effort and carries with it individual responsibility, it is nourished by a vast array of personal associations. This work is no exception. Many people have contributed to this project, but a few must receive special words of appreciation:

—my brother, the Bible scholar, whose gentle questioning prompted the discovery of a key concept crucial to the argument

—my friend, a teacher of children, who laboriously read and perceptively criticized every rough draft

—two strangers, "friends of the mountains," on whom was imposed the first meager outline and who believed in the book for absolutely no good reason at all

—the seminary, whose generous approval of sabbatical made this venture possible

—and my students, who quietly indulged me in my growing enthusiasm about "the book."

D. J. F.

Garrett-Evangelical Theological Seminary
Evanston, Ill.

CONTENTS

Invitation
to
Exploration

Something is wrong with the way the Bible has been taught to children. Church school teachers say so. They complain that Bible units seem difficult to teach and often fail to capture the interest of their class members. Children say so. Fewer and fewer attend church school. Those who do, often forget the biblical facts they learn and carry with them into adolescent years a feeling that Bible study is something for childhood, which they have now outgrown. Adults say so. Although products of the church school, when asked to teach in it they plead biblical ignorance. College professors of religion say so. Each new freshman class regularly brings from the campuses the cry of "biblical illiteracy." And even old-time politicians, their speeches peppered with biblical references, have reason to wonder if they are really understood by their constituents.

There is no simple way to respond to such comments. Suggestions for changing the situation come from many directions. Cognitive psychologists offer a variety of theories about how concepts are formed; learning theorists about how people learn, and educators about how teachers should teach. But psychologists and educators rarely apply their theories to the teaching of the

Bible, preferring to leave this to the church. Bible scholars offer a variety of theories about the nature of the Bible, its basic message, and how it is to be interpreted. But they are usually reluctant to offer suggestions about interpreting the scriptures to children, preferring to leave this to the Christian educators.

It is not surprising that there are feelings of discouragement and frustration. It is even understandable when some church educators retreat into the shelter of indifference and simply give up. On the other hand, sometimes such frustration can produce a surge of creativity which holds within itself the seeds of solution. One kind of creative response to the question of children and the Bible would be to accept the invitation presented in this book to join in yet another exploration for new directions and new understandings.

There are some positive factors present today which should serve as encouragement to those who accept the invitation.

First, there is history. This is not the first such exploration; there are some miles which do not have to be traveled again. For example, the days of treating children as "little adults" are over. Too much has been learned about the unique nature of childhood to demand of children adult behavior and understanding. On the other hand, the days of seeing religious education as "merely character-building" are also over. Too much has been learned about the nature of the Christian gospel to equate morality and Christian faith.

Second, there is a growing concern. An encouraging sign is the renewed interest on the part of adult church members in the subject of teaching the Bible to children.

This is accompanied by a new willingness on the part of denominational curriculum writers and editors to revise teaching materials. Change is possible.

Third, there is the confused situation itself. Although seen as a hopeful sign to only the most optimistic, perhaps, the difficulty and urgency of the task make change more acceptable. The need for a different approach is so obvious that no one needs to be convinced. And dwindling participation in many established programs releases those who might otherwise feel compelled to defend things as they are.

Fourth, there is exploration in other areas of Christian education with children, too. Experimentation with new forms and settings is moving forward at a rapid pace. The image of the traditional Sunday school is no longer either adequate or accurate. New phrases have come into the Christian educator's vocabulary such as "intergenerational," "open classroom," "learning centers," "independent study," "schools without walls," "Tuesday school," and "programmed instruction." This present openness to change in the organizational structure of teaching suggests that there may be willingness to change in other areas—perhaps in the way children are introduced to the Bible.

Feelings of urgency and an uneasy mood of optimism are not enough, however. Explorers learn to navigate by the stars, or they carry a compass, or keep in constant touch with Mission Control—or all three. They need a sense of direction. Their only hope of arriving at their destination is to keep firmly in mind the four points of north, south, east, and west. Instead of four compass points, this exploration into the world of children and the

Bible is based on four Affirmations. These are the assumptions that give direction to the rest of the book.

Affirmation #1: The Bible
In the search for ways to help children discover Bible meanings, the starting point must be an understanding of the nature of the Bible itself.

This exploration begins with an understanding of the Bible and is dependent on the help of sound biblical scholarship. There can be no other place of origin. The Bible is the Christian educator's reason for being. This first affirmation requires that certain questions be answered: Where did the Bible come from? What does it mean to call it the "Word of God"? What does it say? These questions are examined in Section I: The Bible.

Affirmation #2: Children
In the search for ways to help children discover Bible meanings, it is necessary to understand the nature of childhood.

Ways the Bible should be taught to children that are drawn from a study of the Bible must be consistent with what is known about children. To understand children, help is needed from psychologists, biologists, sociologists, and educators. Almost as important, however, teachers must sharpen their own powers of observation and understanding. Questions to ask include: What are children like? How are they limited in their ability to learn? What can they understand about religion? Given the nature of the Bible and the nature of children, how shall the Bible be taught? These are the questions dealt with in Section II: Children and in Section III: Teaching.

Affirmation #3: Discovery of Meaning

This affirmation has two parts. The first is related to the purpose of Bible study for children and hinges on the importance of the word meaning.

The goal of Bible study with children is to help them deal with the "meaning" questions of their lives as they discover meanings in the Bible.

The big question for humanity today is one of finding meaning for life. Everyone works at this problem, including children. For adults, the search prompts questions about life phrased in terms of purpose, ultimacy, significance, direction, destiny, values, relevance, or understanding. If children ask meaning questions they probably do it in the familiar words "Why?" "Why not?" "How come?" "Where to?" and "What for?"

Christians witness to the fact that an experience of the Bible brings new understanding about the meaning of life now. If we allow ourselves to become one of the five thousand who sat at Jesus' feet and eventually expected him to provide food, life may take on a different meaning. We may discover that we, too, are called to be concerned about the needs of other persons. Or, perhaps for the first time, we are forced to contrast the large importance we give to physical needs with the small significance we give to spiritual needs. Or, the most meaningful moment of our life may simply be when we recognize that we, too, want to be counted among those who choose to be followers of Jesus.

The approach to teaching the Bible suggested in Section III: Teaching and the teaching plans offered in Section IV: Models are all intended to help children experience the Bible and through this experience to discover Bible meanings.

The second part of this affirmation relates to the *methods* used in Bible study with children and centers around the word *discover*.

Significant understandings occur when children are actively involved in the teaching-learning process.

Children find meaning through discovery (perhaps even by chance), exploration, investigation, and participation. This is in direct contrast to the notion that "to be told is to know." Methods suggested in Section IV are based on this principle of participation.

The task of teaching children the Bible is essentially one of helping them discover Bible meanings. Together these first three affirmations provide the basis for this task, and they point toward the content of the four major sections of this book. The fourth affirmation is a statement of the organizing principle around which most chapters in Sections I, II, and III are written.

Affirmation #4: Invitation to Exploration
Adults as well as children can find meanings through discovery, exploration, investigation, and participation.

16

Many chapters in Sections I, II, and III are organized to encourage thoughtful participation and decision-making on the part of the reader. Early in these chapters the writer's point of view is concisely stated with no attempt to explain, defend, or convince. The last section of each chapter presents this point of view in more detail. Between the initial statement of the point of view and its expanded explanation, a range of alternative positions has been stated with as much objectivity as possible. After reading each chapter, and in the spirit of exploration, consider and choose the alternative that is most acceptable to you. Include the writer's position as one of the alternatives. In this way, significant insights may be discovered by those who are in total disagreement with the writer—thus proving the truth of Affirmation #4!

Few people are completely satisfied with present efforts to teach children the Bible. In the distant past the unique nature of childhood was ignored, and the Bible was taught as if children were just little adults. In more recent years the starting point has been the nature of the child. Those who begin with the child often emphasize the child's limited ability to understand. The task of the Christian educator thus becomes one of presenting only what can be comprehended while trying to remain true to the nature of the Bible. In contrast, the exploration in this book begins with the Bible itself and the belief that it is important for Christian educators to discover and build on the potential of children, rather than on their limitations.

1.
Bible Beginnings

The story of how the Bible came to be is much more than a series of dates and descriptions of documents, although these are important. Of equal importance is an understanding of the process by which these documents came to be accepted as the Scriptures of the church. This chapter briefly sketches the development of the Bible from the earliest oral traditions to the latest English revisions.

The Oral Tradition

Long before the Bible appeared in written form, many parts of both the Old Testament and the New Testament were passed by word of mouth from village to village and from one generation to the next. Old Testament oral tradition, as it is called, was formed through the repeating of stories or conversations. Some of the stories were about the origins of Israel, the covenant of Israel with God, the Exodus, and the Passover. The liturgical forms of the Old Testament were both part of the oral tradition and carriers of it. Even the laws that came out of the daily life of the community were carried by the oral tradition before they were written into the lawbooks. Before the reign of David, in about the tenth century B.C., there is no evidence of any of this being written down.

Many of the familiar accounts in the New Testament have their origin in an oral tradition also. One of the oldest forms of oral tradition was the *pronouncement story*. When guidance in ethical conduct was needed in the early Christian community, an appropriate personal encounter with Jesus would be recalled and narrated. It would be concluded with a pronouncement to fit the need; for example, "'Render therefore to Caesar the things that are Caesar's, and to God the things that are God's'" (Matthew 22:21).

Another form of the oral tradition was the *miracle story*. When summoning evidence to convince their hearers that Jesus was the Son of God, early Christians would recall stories they had heard of miracles he performed. They would describe the setting and the miraculous act itself. As an ending to the story they would attest to its validity by stating the consequences of the event. For example, the story of the healing of Jairus' daughter concludes with the words, "And immediately the girl got up and walked" (Mark 5:42).

Another of these old forms of the oral tradition was the *sayings of Jesus*. Today we preserve important words with a tape recorder. The followers of Jesus collected his sayings by careful listening and frequent repetition, preserving them in their memories. One of these collections is known to us as the Sermon on the Mount.

The *parables* of Jesus also illustrate a form of oral tradition. Some scholars say that each parable was intended to call attention to a particular truth; others claim that the real purpose of the parables was to hide a truth until people were ready to understand it. For whatever reason, it is clear that the parable was an appealing form, easily remembered, and often repeated. Even today the parables are favorites among children, who frequently choose them as subject matter for dramatization.

Finally, one of the most familiar forms which the oral tradition took was the *stories about Jesus,* including his birth, temptation, transfiguration, death, and resurrection.

Until about A.D. 50 the oral tradition was the only way in which the life of the early Christian community was preserved. This is a significant fact. It means that all the words of Jesus have come to us through this oral tradition. It accounts for the fact that much of the material in the gospels is in short paragraphs and anecdotes which were easy to remember and repeat. Since our Bible carries accounts of only a small fraction of what must have happened, it indicates that the materials so preserved were seen to be of unusual worth. It suggests that interpretations of events and sayings had taken place even before they were written down. Finally, it demonstrates that the roots of the New Testament are deeply imbedded in the life of the early Christian church.

An understanding of the oral tradition does not allow us to view the Bible as a static document from ancient times. Rather, it helps us appreciate it as a dynamic account of living history.

The Written Tradition

Groups that exist long enough to develop self-identity and traditions usually produce historians who in turn produce written records. Somewhere in the line of descendants almost every family has its self-appointed genealogists. Histories are produced by local churches, counties, social groups, and presidents. Ministers gather their sermons into books, and teachers gather their stories into anthologies. It was no different for our Judeo-Christian ancestors. Eventually some of their oral traditions found their way into written form.

It was Old Testament storytellers who first began to gather the rich materials which had been told and retold by women at the wells or by men around the campfires. A storyteller from the south of Judah (called "J" by the Old Testament scholars because he calls God "Jehovah" or "Yahweh") wrote his stories about 850 B.C.

About a hundred years later another storyteller, this time from the north of Judah, put his stories into writing. (He is called "E" because he refers to God as "Elohim.") These two accounts have been woven together and are found in the Pentateuch, the first five books of the Old Testament. Also to be found there are lawbooks of ancient Israel from the fifth and fourth centuries B.C., known as "D" (Deuteronomic Code) and "P" (Priestly Code). Gradually the rest of the Old Testament was added so that by about 200 B.C. all the Old Testament had been written. This was almost seven hundred years after the first known writings. The original language of the Old Testament was Hebrew.

The first written documents of the New Testament are the letters of Paul. Although he must have been familiar with much of the oral tradition, his purpose in writing was not to preserve that tradition. Most of his letters speak directly to the needs of the early Christian churches, especially those in the Gentile world. It is generally agreed that his letter to the Thessalonians is the earliest book in the New Testament, perhaps as early as A.D. 50, and that all of his letters were written before any of the Gospels.

The Gospel of Mark is the earliest written document known to us today which devotes itself to an orderly account of the oral tradition about Jesus. Written about A.D. 65–70, it was followed by Matthew, A.D. 75–85, and Luke, A.D. 85–95. The Gospel of John was written much later, probably between A.D. 100–115.

Both the letters of Paul and the Gospels were intended for those who had not personally known Jesus, because they lived in a distant place or at a later time. They were written in the language of the marketplace, Koine Greek. By A.D. 150 all the New Testament books were in existence.

Canonization

The Bible was written, piece by piece, over a period of almost twelve hundred years. It is certain there were many other religious writings authored during this same period. How some found their way into the Bible and others did not is explained by the term *canonization*. In *A Light to the Nations* (p. 29) Norman K. Gottwald defines canonization as "the process by which sacred books are selected, embued with authority, and thus set apart from other religious writings that are either heretical or simply of devotional value." This selection and setting apart of materials which comprise the Bible occurred in many stages. It was a process that took place both within

Judaism (with reference to the portion we know as the Old Testament) and within the Christian church (with reference to both the Old and New Testaments).

In Judaism, the standard for selection of writings to be given the authority of Scripture seems to have been a practical one. A writing was included if it had been found by common agreement to be useful to those seeking to live a righteous life. The final selection of Jewish writings and the official stamp of approval was by a rabbinic assemby in A.D. 90 at Jamnia, a city west of Jerusalem.

The Christian church from the beginning used the Jewish religious writings. Since the church arose before the Jewish canon was closed, all those books circulating in Judaism before the closing of the canon passed into the church. Thus it became necessary for the church to define the Old Testament canon for itself.

The Old Testament scriptures were used more and more by the church with the conviction that they contained the promise it believed was fulfilled in Jesus Christ. This was understood as their true meaning and intent. So used and interpreted, their acceptance in the Bible of the church was inevitable.

By A.D. 200 there was general agreement that the Gospels, Acts, and Paul's letters were authoritative writings for the Christian. In his Easter letter of A.D. 367, Athanasius, Bishop of Alexandria, listed for the first time the twenty-seven books now found in the New Testament. Since the end of the fourth century this list has been accepted by most parts of the Christian church. The standards used for selection of New Testament writings are not known specifically, but they seem to have included affirmative answers to these three questions: (1)

Was it written by an apostle or someone close to an apostle? (2) Was it used widely by the church in the instruction of converts? (3) Is the authentic tradition presented?

Canonization is the process by which a closed collection of scriptures becomes authorized by the church for use in the churches as the standard for inspiration and teaching.

Translations and Revisions

There are three major incentives for new translations and revisions of the Bible. First is the conviction that all persons should be able to read it in their own language; second is the belief that it is best understood in the contemporary idiom; and third is the never-ending search for increased accuracy in translation. The first two reasons dominated until the nineteenth century. Another surge of interest came with new discoveries of ancient manuscripts and new skill in understanding ancient languages.

Each translation of the Bible and each revision came out of a unique set of circumstances, including technology, politics, doctrinal controversies, and church reform. Men were exiled, some lost their lives, and others lived out their years in fear because they were responsible for new statements of the Bible text. A sweeping look at the development of the English Bible is presented in the chart on pages 26 and 27. Those interested in pursuing this subject can begin by reading "The Making of the English Bible" by Clyde Manschreck in *The Interpreter's One-Volume Commentary on the Bible.*

The journey from oral tradition to the latest edition of the Bible in the English language covers many centuries and depends on countless storytellers, writers, translators, and revisers. In addition to English, the entire Bible has been translated into 243 different languages and dialects. This continued dedication to a difficult task testifies to the vital place the Bible holds in the history of the world.

DEVELOPMENT OF THE ENGLISH BIBLE

Date	Part	Known by What Name?	By Whom?	From What Language and/or Source?	To What Language?	Reason for This Bible	Of Special Interest
270 B.C.	OT	Septuagint	Jewish Scholars	Hebrew	Greek	Many Jews could no longer read Hebrew accurately	Traditionally 70 men translated it, giving it its name
A.D. 385-405	OT-NT	Vulgate	Jerome	Hebrew and Greek	Latin	Into language of the people	Official Roman Catholic translation, commissioned by the Pope
1380-1382	OT-NT	Lollard Bible	John Wycliffe, Nicholas Hereford	Latin Vulgate	English	Into language of the people	First complete English translation
1525	NT	Tyndale Bible	William Tyndale	Erasmus' Greek New Testament	English	Into language of the people	First English Bible based on original language
1535	OT-NT	Coverdale Bible	Miles Coverdale	Tyndale's English, Luther's German, Vulgate	English	Need for a complete English Bible	First complete English Bible
1539	OT-NT	The Great Bible	Miles Coverdale	Tyndale, Coverdale Bibles	English	A Bible suitable for use in every parish church	First authorized version; name derived from size
1560	OT-NT	Geneva Bible	John Knox, William Whittingham, Miles Coverdale	Hebrew, Luther's German, and all available sources	English	Marginal notes and language to reflect Calvinistic doctrine	First English Bible to designate verses

26

Year		Version	Translator/Authority	Revision of Great Bible / Source	Language	Need/Reason	Notes
1568	OT-NT	The Bishop's Bible	Church of England	Revision of Great Bible	English	Need for a Bible without Calvinistic interpretation and notes	Second authorized version
1611	OT-NT	King James Version	Church of England committee of scholars	Original documents and all available English translations	English	To unify the Church of England	Third authorized version
1885	OT-NT	English Revised Version	"	"	English	Accuracy, on basis of discovery of new documents	Edited in 1901 in America and published as the American Standard version. Fourth authorized version
1946-1952	OT-NT	Revised Standard Version	ICRE/NCC,* committee of scholars	"	English	Accuracy, on basis of new discoveries, and English usage	Fifth authorized version
1961-1970	OT-NT	The New English Bible	Protestant groups in British Isles	"	English	Accuracy; English usage	A new translation, not a revision
1966	OT-NT	The Jerusalem Bible	Dominican Biblical School, Jerusalem	Hebrew and Greek	French and English	Need for scholarly work in contemporary English	A study Bible with notes
1970	OT-NT	The New American Bible	CCD,** Roman Catholic Church	All available sources	English		

*International Council of Religious Education/National Council of Churches.
**CCD—Confraternity of Christian Doctrine.

2.
A Confronting Event

Point of View:
The Bible is a written witness to experiences of Divine-human encounter in the past and is an Event through which Divine-human encounter is possible in the present.

The Bible is central to our understanding of Christianity. The earliest Christians possessed the Old Testament in the form of the Jewish Scriptures. From the very beginning the church knew the valuable oral traditions about the life, death, and resurrection of Jesus. The letters of Paul were read in the churches less than twenty-five years after the death of Jesus. And by A.D. 150 all the writings in the Bible were available.

Throughout all the centuries that followed, people have tried to adequately describe the nature of the Bible, and the resulting interpretations of its meaning have been many. These varied approaches have led to numerous theological positions, hundreds of denominations and sects, a wide range of life-styles, and even bitter conflict between Christians. In spite of all these differences, Christians have given general consent to a description of the Bible, calling it "the Word of God." We recognize that the Bible is uniquely a book about God, but the question remains, in what way is it the Word of God?

28

This chapter examines six different descriptions of the nature of the Bible. Five are perspectives readily discovered in the course of general Bible study. The sixth is the writer's point of view. In writing about each of the first five approaches there is brief mention of how it influences the way the Bible is taught to children and of its major contributions.

Some Other Perspectives

The Bible as God's Word: Written and Uninterpreted

Some who describe the Bible as the Word of God use the term in a literal sense. That is, the Bible contains the actual words of God, faithfully and accurately recorded by the writers. Since God's revelation is through these words, the exact terminology of the biblical text becomes extremely important. Revisions are seen as interpretations and therefore a tampering with the Scriptures. Efforts are not made to understand the text in terms of cultural and historical roots. It is felt that the Word of God can be known through the Bible—and in no other way. Some have a less literal approach, but still want to be sure that the Bible as the revelation of God is allowed to speak without interpretation.

When this view of the Bible is held by teachers of children, a certain teaching style emerges. First, the importance of the text itself leads to an emphasis on memorization of Bible verses. These are often chosen for their brevity or ease in memorization. Second, the importance of the text is sometimes interpreted to mean that all portions of the Bible are equally relevant. It is felt that children can learn a lesson from almost any portion of the

Bible. Third, in the use of Bible stories the emphasis is on the details of the story and perhaps its moral application. Fourth, the Bible is sometimes seen as the only text necessary.

A major contribution of those who hold this view is their firm stand that the Bible is unique, that it is the primary source for our understanding of God, and as such it is essential for Christian faith.

The Bible as an Interpretation of God's Word

The Bible is declared to be God's Word by many who do not hold the view just described. These people acknowledge that *interpretation* of the Bible has occurred since the beginning of the oral tradition. In repeating a story or idea over and over again interpretive words crept in. As persons translated from Hebrew and Greek to Latin and then to several English editions over a period of more than four hundred years, they left in the text traces of their own understanding. Citing Jeremiah 1:1-2, "The Words of Jeremiah . . . to whom the word of the Lord came," one writer suggests that the Bible is "the word of men seeking to express the Word of God which has come to them."

Others qualify their concept of the Bible as the Word of God by saying it is a *record* of God's Word or that it *contains* God's Word. Even though interpretation by storytellers, writers, and translators is conceded, there is still the hope that interpretation may be kept to a minimum. In the effort to recover original texts, the skills of biblical scholarship are employed.

When applied to the teaching of children this view puts emphasis on Bible knowledge, although not necessarily the ability to recall the precise words of the text. Stories and larger segments such as the Ten Commandments, Sermon on the Mount, and parables are stressed rather than single verses. To understand the text itself it is thought helpful to have an understanding of the writers, their audience, and the cultural and historical setting in which they lived. Therefore, in addition to the Bible, children use supplementary resources such as maps, concordances, commentaries, and pupils' books containing other background materials.

The major contribution of those who hold this view is the freedom from strict adherence to the text that is possible because of the conviction that Bible writers and translators included some of their own understanding.

The Bible as a Sourcebook

Some who refer to the Bible as a *sourcebook* see it as a book about human beings rather than a book about God. To call it the Word of God is to set it apart from other books. Its uniqueness lies in the particular set of events it describes, not in the special quality of the events.

As a sourcebook the Bible has value for Christians and non-Christians alike. To the extent that its events and dates can be scientifically verified, the Bible is of interest to historians and political scientists. Sociologists and anthropologists study its tribal organization, religious rites, descriptions of villages and cities, and customs and mores of its people. Students of literature and language development appreciate it as an important resource. According to one Bible scholar, those who use the Bible in these ways see it as a "literary artifact to unlock the mystery of the times."

Others see the Bible as a unique sourcebook for Christians. It not only contains information about the past, but provides answers to the problems of living in today's world. Although some would say that answers to all questions can be found in the Bible and that no other source is necessary, most would agree that the Bible is only one of many sources to which persons may go to find solutions for problems. In either case, the Bible is read as one would read an encyclopedia rather than as one would read a story.

There are two ways church school teachers use the Bible as a sourcebook. Those who see it as a source for rules of conduct and answers to life's problems make frequent reference to the Ten Commandments, the Golden Rule, the Sermon on the Mount, and selections from the letters of Paul. Sometimes a Bible reference will open up discussion of a child's question or problem. More often the immediate need is discussed first, and then a commonsense solution is found and validated by reference to the Bible. Teachers who see the Bible as only one resource book among many use it to stimulate thinking, give information, and provide one perspective which can then be compared with others. In this case many other reference books are made available to be used in the same way. Since it is a sourcebook, children are taught how to find portions of the Bible they wish to use.

A major contribution of the sourcebook view is the conviction that Bible study simply for its own sake is not enough. For the Bible to have any meaning for the reader it must speak to a need for information or deal with some of life's persistent concerns.

The Bible as a History of God's People

The ordinary people of Israel became extraordinary as they came to see themselves as God's people. The Bible is sometimes described as a history of God's people. It is seen as an account of important people and events, often replete with specific dates and places. Unlike the source-book view, however, this history is unique because through it God has made himself known.

The history of the Judeo-Christian tradition is of special interest to Christians, perhaps in the same way that study of American history is of interest to Americans. To maintain our identity as a nation, it is important that we be reminded from time to time of our historical origins. References might be made to the American Revolution, the Constitution, and the words of Washington and Jefferson. Similarly, Christianity is better understood when people are reminded of the Creation, the Exodus, the words of the Prophets, the birth, death, and resurrection of Jesus, and the beginnings of the Christian church.

The Bible is seen as unique history, however, because through this history God has revealed himself. God's word was spoken to a particular group of people, at a particular time, and within a particular cultural setting. God's word is the same now as it was then. Therefore, through the understanding and interpretation of this history, God's word is known to us today.

Those who teach from this view have a special interest in Bible customs, geography, and the sequence of events. Anxious that children know Bible customs, they display Bible pictures that have been painted only after careful research or help children make Palestinian villages.

If drama is used, care is taken to make costumes, scenic background, and props as authentic as possible. Because a knowledge of the geography is necessary, map study is carried out using wall charts, atlases, globes, or detailed relief maps made by the children. Since the sequence of historical events is important, children learn dates, places, and names by memorization or by the creation of time lines.

One major contribution of this approach is the conviction that to really understand the Bible it is necessary to have an understanding of the cultural and historical setting in which it was written.

The Bible as a Witness to Divine-Human Encounter

Three of the four concepts of the Bible which have been presented so far describe God as the most active participant in the Divine-human relationship. In these views God spoke to the people of Israel through the events of their history, and he speaks to us today through the written record of these events in the Bible. The expectation of response on the part of God's listeners has not been obvious although it may have been implied.

Viewing the Bible as a *witness* to Divine-human encounter brings forth three new elements of its nature.

First, it introduces the human being as an active participant in God's history. The concern is not only with the Word, but with human response to that Word. The Bible is not only a book about God; it is a book about the way people have responded to God.

Second, this approach to the Bible introduces the dimension of encounter. An encounter between two persons is not usually a casual meeting, although the dictionary gives that as one meaning of the word. It is more often an intense relationship which is not quickly forgotten. It is a give-and-take in which each makes demands on the other with such insistence that they cannot be ignored. The Bible tells of this kind of interaction and struggle between God and persons. It is more than a history of events. And it is more than God speaking and people responding. The Bible is a witness to Divine-human encounter.

The third new element in this approach is indicated by the word "witness." The Bible was written by witnesses to this history of encounter between God and people. Because the witnesses were participants in the encounter, it cannot be an objective history. They interpreted God's Word in the light of their own response to that Word.

An understanding of the Bible as a witness to Divine-human encounter adds new possibilities for the teacher of children. Since the people of the Bible themselves take on added significance, the teacher plans activities that will make these people come alive. Many of the activities used by those who view the Bible as a "history of God's people" are just as appropriate here. But time lines, pictures, maps, and Palestinian villages cannot adequately describe what it is like to have an encounter with God! The teacher is interested in helping children understand the feelings of Bible persons. For example, the parable of the prodigal son might be acted out with an emphasis on the emotional responses of the characters. Or children might make puppets and use them to portray the feelings of the Wise Men and the shepherds.

The first purpose of all these activities is to help children know how it felt to be the human side of the

Divine-human encounter. The second purpose is to help children discover what the people of the Bible learned about God. This is seen by some to be the most important result of the teaching because it is through the experiences of Bible persons that we know what God is like.

The major contribution of this approach is the conviction that the Bible is not a book just about God, but that it is a book about the encounter between God and persons, written by witnesses who were also participants.

The Bible: A Confronting Event

The concept of the Bible as a *confronting event* does not stand in total opposition to the five views just presented, but it builds on the major contributions of each. While leaning most heavily on the understanding of the Bible as a witness to Divine-human encounter, it adds elements of its own.

The Bible Is an Event

There is a difference between talking about the "events" recorded in the Bible and describing the Bible as an "event." The events in the Bible are sometimes observable bits of history such as battles, births, deaths, shipwrecks, political intrigues, famines, floods, or baptisms. Sometimes these events are persons: Abraham, Isaac, Jacob, Moses, the prophets, the disciples, Jesus Christ, or Paul. Sometimes events are interpreted in such a meaningful way that the interpretations themselves become events—for example, the stories of Creation, the messages of the prophets, the pronouncements of the Gospel writers, or the theology of Paul. Sometimes events are experiences or happenings such as the conversion of Paul or

Jacob's dream. It is through these events and others like them that God has made himself known.

In the same way that a letter from Paul was an event in the lives of the early Christians who heard it read in the churches, the Bible can be an event in the lives of Christians today. Although it is sixty-six distinct books and therefore might properly be referred to as sixty-six events, the church has selected them as uniquely valuable for Christians. These books, together known to us as the Bible, have become one book with its own identity and its own life. This book gathers up all the events recorded in each of the books, and, as a collection of history, interpretations, persons, and experience, it becomes itself another event to be understood, another event through which persons can discover God. And because it is synonymous with the Bible, we spell this event with a capital E, and call the Bible an Event.

The Bible Is a "Now" Event

The first five perspectives described the Bible largely in the past tense. The Bible contains words written long ago; it tells of events that occurred in another age; it is a sourcebook which contains a history of an ancient people; it witnesses to Divine-human encounters that took place in the past.

We limit the Bible if we see it only as a record of something that happened long ago. As an Event it has within itself the power to bring the past into the present in such a spectacular way that the Bible becomes a "now" Event in the lives of persons today. It is an Event through which God seeks to make himself known to us just as he did through the events of the past to which it witnesses.

The Bible Brings About Encounter

It is the testimony of Christians through the ages that the Bible is not something that can be taken or left alone. Just as the events recorded in the Bible confronted the people who participated in them, so the Bible as an Event confronts us here and now. The Bible is not only a record of Divine-human encounters in the past, but by its very nature it has the power to bring God and persons together in encounters today. When we willingly open ourselves to it, we risk opening to ourselves, to one another, and to God in such a way that we cannot escape a Divine-human encounter. Because the Bible brings about Divine-human encounter, it can be called a "confronting" Event.

The Bible: A Channel for God's Word

The idea of the Bible as the Word of God is so much a part of the history of the Christian church that it must be dealt with in some way by everyone who attempts to describe its nature. Some people see the Bible text itself as the Word of God; others find God's Word in an interpretation of the events of history; still others discover it in the midst of the Divine-human encounters written about in the Bible.

If the Bible is best described as a confronting Event, how is this Event to be understood as the Word of God? Many have struggled with the question, Does a tree falling in a forest make any sound if no one is there to hear it fall? We know that falling trees make a noise because we have the word of those who have been there. To wonder about the presence of sound in the absence of hearers is an intriguing question, but for most of us the answer leads to no important consequence. The crucial observation to make about falling trees is the fact that if we are in the forest when one falls, we jump! And as we jump we say, "What a noise that makes!" Our experience in the forest will make it very difficult for us to ever imagine a tree falling in utter silence.

Is the Bible the Word of God if no one reads it or if it is read as only history or a sourcebook? It is the testimony of the Christian church that in some way it can be understood to be God's Word. To debate what it means to call it the Word of God is for most of us an empty exercise. The crucial observation about the Bible lies in the fact that if we approach it in such a way that we allow it to confront us, we must respond. And one way we respond is to say, "Surely the Bible must be the Word of God!" Our experience with the Bible will make it very difficult for us to ever think about it without in some way describing it as God's Word.

God and persons have been engaged in confrontation and response since the beginning of the human race. Some of the witnesses to these events have written their observations and interpretations. These reflections, along with other writings, were selected by the church to become its authorized Scriptures. The Bible not only describes events of Divine-human encounter in the past, but is itself a confronting Event which can enable persons today to enter into meaningful relationships with God. And those who respond when confronted experience it to be for them the Word of God.

More difficult than describing the nature of the Bible is the task of answering the question: Can the Bible be for children a confronting Event? And if so, how?

39

3.
Unlimited Meanings

Point of View:
The Bible says to everyone, "Here I am! In me there
is the possibility of meaning for you! Discover it!"

The search for an adequate statement of the Bible message is a constant one. To say that the Bible is a confronting Event describes its nature, but it says nothing about
the message one can expect to receive because of the
confrontation that has taken place. The question crying to
be answered is, What does the Bible say? In an effort to
voice their understanding of the Bible, some have tried to
discover a central theme that runs throughout the entire
book. There is no unanimous agreement, however, about
such a theme because persons bring to their study of the
Bible their own past experiences, their own needs, and
their own religious beliefs. Those who do agree on a
central theme often have widely varying interpretations
of its meaning. This is no cause for surprise or anxiety.
The Bible writers themselves understood and interpreted
the events of their times in different ways. The unity of
the Bible is to be found in its witness that Divine-human
encounter is possible, not in a single explanation of what
this encounter means.

In the section that follows, three biblical themes are
presented, along with a few of the ways each has been
interpreted and some of the ways each might affect the

method by which children are taught the Bible. In the concluding section of this chapter the writer shares her own approach to the question, What does the Bible say?

All four statements stand within the Christian tradition. No one of them should be seen as right or wrong, but together they give additional evidence that the Bible holds meaning for those who allow themselves to be confronted by it.

Some Bible Themes

People Are in Trouble

This people-are-in-trouble theme is found in both the Bible and the modern world. The psalmist commented,

> The Lord looks down from heaven
>   upon the children of men.
>   to see if there are any that act wisely,
>   that seek after God.
> They have all gone astray, they are all
>   alike corrupt;
>   there is none that does good
>   no, not one (Psalm 14:2-3).

In the midst of World War II, Elton Trueblood wrote, "Something has gone wrong with our civilization." He called the problem and his book *The Predicament of Modern Man*. Although many see this same predicament as a central theme of the Bible, they often describe it in different ways.

Some say that people are in trouble because they are sinners in need of salvation. This is a theological way of talking about the predicament. One view is that people are born good, but that by their actions or the influence of

41

a corrupt society they fall away and become sinners. Another view is that all people are born sinners and can be nothing else. In either case, the way out of the dilemma is only through God's salvation.

Others say people are in trouble because of alienation. We are alienated from one another through personal misunderstandings. Pollution, space travel, energy crises, crime, and nuclear wars have made us feel like aliens in our world. Perhaps more seriously, we are even alienated from ourselves. These are psychological explanations of our predicament. We are in need of reconciliation, wholeness, and mental health; one writer calls this need "wholth."

Still others would remind us that being in trouble is the story of our collective lives. In his play *The Skin of Our Teeth*, Thornton Wilder portrays with humor the struggle for survival that has gone on ever since the creation of the world. Whenever the human race has just about extricated itself from the ashes of a great calamity, a new catastrophe befalls it! So we have gone from famine to flood to plague to war to who knows what will happen next? This is a historical explanation of our predicament. Somehow we need to find a way to break out of this pattern.

Our understanding of the predicament theme, both its importance and its meaning, will influence the goals and teaching methods used in the Christian education of children. If sinfulness is stressed, the Bible may be used as a doorway to conversion or as a set of "Thou shalt nots." If alienation is the interpretation chosen, there may be more importance placed on the quality of the interpersonal relationships between teachers and children than on the quantity of Bible material. If our predicament is seen largely as a struggle for survival, there will in all likelihood be an emphasis on community, national, and worldwide concerns.

Although interpretations of its meaning vary, the people-are-in-trouble theme is widely held as central to the biblical message.

God Acts in History

The people-are-in-trouble theme focuses its attention on the plight and activity of persons. In contrast, God is the central figure for those who say the Bible can be understood best if we see it as a testimony that God has acted throughout our history. To say this is to dispute some other popular notions about God. For instance, emphasis on the activity of God in history is a denial of the idea that at the time of creation God wound up the world and then turned it loose to run on its own. Nor is it possible to see God as a judge who sits apart watching the activities of people, immobile until appealed to for help. Rather, the Bible is a record of God's ongoing creative activity in the world. The fact that he has acted in history is important because we can assume that he is active in our history too.

Those who contend that God's action in history is the central theme of the Bible characterize this action through a variety of descriptive terms. Only two will be mentioned.

First, there are those who see God as active in the "saving events" of our Judeo-Christian tradition. This obviously builds on the people-are-in-trouble theme since people need to be rescued from personal or cosmic disaster. These saving events include, among others, God's call and his promises to Abraham, his deliverance of Israel from slavery, and the life, death, and resurrection of Jesus Christ. The emphasis here is on particular events in which we see God's saving activity.

Second, there are those who stress not only the events themselves, but the relationship between these events—the dependency they have on one another. Bernhard Anderson, in his book, *The Unfolding Drama of the Bible*, has given us the imagery of God's action in history as a historical drama with three acts. The use of drama ties the events together with a beginning and an ending. God is the central figure in the play. He is the Director, the Prompter in the wings, and the Chief Actor on the stage. The "program" looks like this:

Prologue: Creation
    Act I:
        Scene 1—Encounter with God
        Scene 2—Discipline and Disaster
    Act II:
        Scene 1—The Second Exodus
        Scene 2—People of the Law
    Act III:
        Scene 1—Victory Through Defeat
        Scene 2—Church and World
Epilogue: History's Finale

The drama of the Bible begins with Creation and rapidly unfolds as other events follow. In act I, scene 1, the encounter of God with his people takes place in the events of the Exodus, in his call to Moses, in the covenant promise, and in the designation of the Jews as his chosen people. Scene 2 describes the rise and fall of Israel and God's judgment of his people. Act II, scene 1 tells the story of the Babylonian exile and the deliverance from it by God's action. The response in terms of becoming the "people of the Law" is shown in scene 2. The climax of the drama is in act III, scene 1. Here the Christ event is depicted as victory through defeat. The results of this victory appear in scene 2. They are Pentecost, God's new creation—the church—and the beginnings of the gospel spread into all the world. The epilogue is the affirmation that the biblical drama has been moving toward a goal and that the goal is the working out of God's purpose in the world. It is in the epilogue that we catch a vision of the coming kingdom of God, a time when persons are restored to the "peace, unity, and blessedness" which God intends for them.

Variations of this theme are possible by choosing one of the events as a theme within a theme. For example, another way of speaking of God's action in history is to refer specifically to the covenant relationship written about in Exodus 24:7-8 and then to interpret the entire Bible as the working out of this covenant.

If the Bible is primarily a guide to understanding that God works in history, teachers will not teach the Bible as isolated bits of fact. Rather, they will help children grasp the broad outline of Bible history, stressing at each point God's activity. In addition they will interpret the Bible as evidence that God continues to be active in the affairs of the world today. One group of denominations highlights its understanding of how God works in history by calling its teaching-learning materials the "Covenant Life Curriculum."

Whether understood as saving events, an unfolding drama, or the story of a promise, the common theme is that God has been and continues to be active in all of history.

God Acts Uniquely Through Jesus Christ

The message of the Bible is understood in yet another way. The Bible is not merely evidence that God acts in history, but it is first and foremost a declaration that in the historic events surrounding the person of Jesus, God acted in a unique way. Some people refer to this cluster of events as the "Christ event." So important is this Christ event that the Bible cannot be understood apart from it. The Old Testament is building toward it and must be interpreted in its light. The New Testament owes its existence to it.

The centrality of Jesus Christ to the New Testament and to the Christian faith is unquestioned. How he is the central theme of the Old Testament is less obvious, but can be understood best if the drama imagery is used again. In this case, Jesus Christ is the main character. To leave the theater at the end of act I would be to hear God's promise, but miss the most amazing way in which the promise was fulfilled—in the person of Jesus. To leave the theater at the end of act II would be to witness the deliverance of the Jews from slavery in Babylon, only to see them become slaves of their own preoccupation with the law. It is only in act III that their ultimate source of freedom is revealed. Through acts I and II (the Old Testament), players and audience alike know the script. They have seen the "cast of characters in the order of their appearance" and know that the eventual coming of a Messiah or "savior" is in act III. It is this faith with

46

which the actors in the first two acts live and interpret the events of their history.

This theme offers a wealth of biblical materials for use in teaching children. There are stories told by Jesus, especially the parables, and there are the collections of his sayings. There are the stories told about Jesus—stories of his birth, his family, his work, his travels, his friends, his relationship to the religious leaders of his time, and his death and resurrection. Some teachers combine this theme with the people-are-in-trouble theme and stress the saving nature of Christ through whom God is acting now. Here the Bible may be used to impress upon children the urgency of commitment. Others combine this with the God-acts-in-history theme and underscore the fact that God acted by creating Jesus, a real person, who lived at a particular time and did and taught certain specific things. These teachers may use the Bible to show that we can learn how to live as Christians by observing how he lived and learning from what he taught.

If people are in trouble, and if God acts through history, then God acting through Jesus Christ to save the people is a summary of the Bible message, and Jesus Christ is the embodiment of that message.

The Bible: Unlimited Meanings

When the question is asked, "What does the Bible say?" it is usually assumed that the answer will be given as if the question had been, "What does the Bible say to everyone in every age?" Or perhaps a note of "ought-ness" creeps in when the answer is given as if the original question had been, "What should everyone hear the Bible say?" A better approach might be to divide the question into two parts: First, "What does the Bible say to everyone?" and second, "What does the Bible say to me?" The rest of this chapter addresses itself to these two questions.

What the Bible Says to Everyone

There are some who seek to answer the question in terms of a single, definitive theme. These attempts can be helpful as contributions to our thinking, although universal acceptance of any one of them is unlikely. Even if such agreement were possible, there are good reasons why it should not be our goal. In the first place, the writers of the Bible ought to be allowed to speak for themselves. To interpret their words under the umbrella of some overarching theme may be to impose upon them a point of view with which they would not agree. Rather than limiting their witness in this way, we should rejoice in the richness of their diverse testimony which, taken as a whole, becomes an Event with power to engage us in an encounter with God.

In the second place, times change. Although the Bible is a timeless document, it is understood differently at different times. In the early part of this century the possibility of a people-are-in-trouble theme was quite remote. It did not become popular until the sobering experiences of the Great Depression followed almost immediately by World War II. We have not been bound by past interpretations of the Bible message; similarly, future generations will not allow us to limit their understanding by insistence on one particular theme.

All this is not to say that the Bible does not "speak." It

is only to say that its message is in the form of an invitation rather than a final statement. The Bible says to everyone, "Here I am! In me there is possibility of meaning for you! Discover it!" An affirmative answer to this invitation indicates our willingness to be confronted by the Bible. As we respond to that confrontation the meanings we each discover belong to us in a special way. They need not, and probably will not, be expressed in the same way as meanings discovered by others. But it is the personal ownership of the meaning that gives it enough vitality so that it can make a difference in our lives.

There is a danger that this kind of approach to the discovery of Bible meanings will become too individualistic. It is necessary that we avoid falling into the trap of saying, "It doesn't matter what you believe, just so you believe something." This is less likely to happen if emerging understandings are explored and tested in the company of others who have embarked on the same search. It is appropriate, therefore, that the Christian community be the place where we hear and respond to the invitation to discover biblical meanings. The Bible grew out of the witness of the early Christian community; the writings preserved in our Bible were selected by this community; the Christian community, therefore, can serve as a corrective to personal interpretations.

Another Bible Meaning: The "For Us-ness" of God

If the answer to the first question ("What does the Bible say to everyone?") is "Here I am—discover my meaning," how shall we answer the second question, "What does the Bible say to me?" Simply to restate the conviction that each person must discover the meaning for himself/

herself and thus bypass the question altogether would be a cop-out. Therefore, in addition to the three themes previously described, the writer offers a fourth theme. Whatever statement the reader makes in response to the question will become a possible fifth theme.

The Bible clearly affirms that God is *for* us. Throughout the succession of events recorded in the Bible, his active concern for all persons is made plain. It takes many forms but shows itself primarily in the ways God acts. He gives, withholds, takes away; he threatens, pleads, punishes, approves, shows mercy, loves. And he does all this because he has high hopes for us; he has confidence in us. He is for us and against anything that diminishes us. Even when we really foul things up the reality of God's "for us-ness" holds out to us the possibility of new life.

Jesus Christ is the most dramatic evidence of God's "for us-ness." He is both the messenger and the message. It is as if God has pulled out all the stops at once in his efforts to convince us of our own worthiness.

Admittedly this is an optimistic point of view, but the Bible is an optimistic book. It witnesses to the fact that God is devoted to developing the potential of his people.

God's past actions have been witnessed to by the Bible writers. But God still acts among us. We, too, are witnesses to his activity in the world. There are meanings still to be discovered. It is valid to look at both our history and our present in the search for these meanings. It is important to open the Bible to children in such a way that the past holds out meanings for the present and possibilities of new meanings in the future.

1.
Children in a Changing World

There are two major factors in the development of every child. First is the being itself that is born into the world. It comes with some physical characteristics already determined by the genes inherited from its parents. It arrives equipped with a sexual identity and a racial identity. But at the moment of birth, it encounters the world and the expectations with which it must learn to cope.

While in broad terms it is the same world for all children, in reality each child is born into a particular world, different from that belonging to anyone else. A first child lives in a very different family, for instance, from the brother or sister born several years later. The interplay between this unique being and its unique world makes it inevitable that each child will develop in his or her own unique way.

There is a possibility, however, that today's children are not only unique as individuals in relation to one another, but that as a generation they are unique from every other generation of children that has ever lived, because the world into which they were born is so strikingly different from the world of any other generation.

It is important to realize that children are not duplicating the experiences of other generations. To preface a

51

statement about behavior with the admonition "When I was your age . . ." is no longer appropriate (if it ever was!), because in a very real sense adults today never were "their age."

There are those who will protest that the world is always in the process of transition, and in this respect today's children are no different from the young of any era. Yet almost every bone of society's body aches as it never has before from the pressure of rapid change. We may be too close to these changes and too personally involved to fully understand either the causes or the results. A descriptive and comparative word picture of how it seems may be the best we can do.

An Unknown Future

The unpredictability of the future may be one of the most significant ways in which our world differs from other times. Margaret Mead points out that a few generations ago children could visualize their future adulthood by watching their grandparents. Now parents and grandparents find their own life-styles influenced by the lifestyles of the young. The continuity between past and future seems to be broken, resulting in an uncertain present and an unpredictable future.

Society's Institutions Are Questioned

It has been customary for sociologists to cite three primary institutions of society: the family, the church, and the school. The structures and values of these institutions provided the stability which made orderly change possible. Although each of them has undergone radical reconstruction from time to time, it is difficult to recall another period when all three have been called into question simultaneously.

The Family

For many children the unity of extended or nuclear families has been replaced by divided families or single-parent homes. For some young adults the concept of legal marriage itself is being questioned. Others have discovered in communal living a new kind of extended family. When talking about family today, no particular organization of persons can be assumed.

The Church

The church, too, is feeling the pressure of change. A church building may stand at the center of some towns and villages, but rarely is it still the center around which the entire community life is organized. Although there have always been critics outside the church, more and more they seem to be within the institution itself.

The Public School

Finally, the institution of the public school is being challenged by both professional educators and local citizens. Criticism with a view to improving the schools is not new. What is new is the serious suggestion that the whole concept of schooling as we know it may be ineffective in today's world and, therefore, obsolete. The best known interpretation of this point of view is in *Deschooling Society* by Ivan Illich.

Violence: A Way of Life

Until recent years, violence was something that happened someplace else to someone else. Wars were fought abroad. Now, through the miracle of television, they are fought nightly in the living rooms and dining rooms of our country. The same newscasts bring vivid word and picture descriptions of violence close at hand. While violence is viewed by some children on television only, other children are experiencing it firsthand. Guns are purchased by children, and murders committed by fourteen-year-olds are becoming more frequent. Children and adults alike seem to have become immune to the horrors of violence.

People Come in Many Colors

Only a few short years ago all American children lived in a white world, acknowledged to be so by those of all races. Today children live in a multicolored world. Through the efforts of the black community, black children are learning to say and feel the words, "Black is beautiful!" Children in Mexican, Puerto Rican, Indian, and other communities are gaining new respect for their history and origins, and white children are learning this, too. White is no longer considered best, nor is it a mark of Christian virtue to say, "I never notice a person's color; I only see the person." In today's world, to see persons is to see their color. Few parents and teachers have any personal experience with which to help children cope with the demands that these changes bring.

Changing Sex Roles

"Little boys grow up to be fathers who leave home every morning and go to work. Little girls grow up to be mothers who stay home, take care of the house and the children, and wait for father to come home to dinner." Until very recently this statement would have gone unchallenged as an idea, if not a reality. But there is a new wind blowing today, and in some places that wind is reaching gale proportions. Where wives engage in work outside the home, more and more husbands are accepting a share of the child-care and household responsibilities. Many women are no longer satisfied with the secretarial, teacher, or nurse image of the employed woman, but aspire to positions of management and acceptance in traditionally male vocations such as truck drivers, police officers, or ordained ministers. In turn, men are freer to become nurses, kindergarten teachers, or secretaries. Although the effects of this trend cannot be fully predicted, there is no doubt that it will have a profound influence on children growing up today.

Life-Work Concept Obsolete

"What are you going to be when you grow up?" is no longer an appropriate way to begin a conversation with a child. With changing technology and social structures, children cannot know the variety of occupations that will be available to them when they are ready to join the work force. Furthermore, if the question is posed at all, it would be more accurate to ask, "What are you going to be *first* when you grow up? And then what? And then what?"

The same forces in society which create new occupations can now make current occupations obsolete within the lifetime of an individual. Men who began their careers as test pilots learned new skills so that they could meet the challenges of space as astronauts. Many of these men, because of budget cutbacks by the federal government, are finding the third career of their lifetime in the private sector. The child of today who says "I'm going to be a librarian and an engineer and a computer programmer" may not be indecisive—just realistic.

The World Is Getting Bigger

Through modern transportation and communication techniques, the time it takes to reach the other side of the globe, or to convey a message across thousands of miles, has been shortened. Rather than having a small part of the world with which to deal, children must now come to terms in some way with the entire world, including both the earth and all it contains and the space in which it rides. It is no longer possible to withhold information from a child for presentation at some later, more appropriate time.

The Knowledge Explosion

If the right questions were chosen for a test in any subject, the most learned scholar in the field would make a poor showing. Information in every area is being amassed at such a rapid rate it is impossible for one person to know everything about anything, let alone know a great deal about everything. In spite of this, most educational systems are still built on the premise that the retention of information is the primary goal. For children experiencing the knowledge explosion, this is a goal that can lead only to frustration. Although information will always be valuable, and some absolutely necessary, the ability to retrieve information from libraries and computers will be even more important. Persons in this new world can no longer be expected to be storehouses of all knowledge. They must learn how to use other storehouses.

Church school teachers of children are often asked to get down on their knees in order to see a classroom from the eye level of a child. If we cannot grow up in the children's world, the least we can do is try to understand the world in which they are growing up.

2.
Understanding Today's Children

Point of View:
Today's children are strangers, wanting and waiting
to be known.

If we take the fact of a changing world seriously, we are faced with a dilemma, because the most quoted theories that describe what children are like were developed in a pre-Space Age, pre-Electronic Age, and most in the pre-Atomic Age. Can we be sure that these theories describe the children of today's world? The need may be for new theories to be developed on the basis of research done in a new world.

In the meantime there is much we can learn from the research of the twentieth century and from our own careful observations of the children we know. The rest of this chapter reviews some of the things we know about children in general, although they may not be precisely true for any child in particular.

Childhood in Developmental Terms

Almost since its beginning this has been called the "century of the child." In the first decade, graded curriculum materials for religious education were introduced, built on the newly acquired conviction that children's needs and abilities were different at different ages.

There was an optimistic attitude that the problem of teaching children and preparing them to take their place in society could be solved if we could know exactly what made a child "tick." As a result, extensive research projects were undertaken. Experimental schools were established where theories could be tried and results could be measured.

Some of the classical theorists of this century are John Dewey, Arnold Gesell, Erik Erikson, Robert Havighurst, and Jean Piaget. Even though they used different research methods and described their findings in different terms, they all agree on one important principle: Human growth is best described in developmental terms.

The Developmental Process

As persons mature, the changes that take place occur in an orderly fashion, each building on the last. These are referred to as developmental stages or tasks or steps. Although the rate of growth may vary, the sequence or pattern of change remains the same. Even the variation in rate of change is thought to be small enough that generalizations are often made in terms of specific age groups. This made it possible for Gesell to talk about the "terrible two's" and the "trusting three's" and for books to contain chapters with titles such as "The Kindergarten Years," "Characteristics of Early Elementary Children," or "What Juniors Are Like."

In the area of physical growth it is easy to see the developmental process at work. Before children can learn to walk they must master a series of other tasks. In sequence these include learning to sit with support, to sit alone, to stand with help, to stand while holding to something, to creep, to walk when led, and to stand alone. Only when this last task has been accomplished are they ready to take their first solo steps. Developmental theorists assert that this sequence of events is inherent in the nature of persons and, therefore, is descriptive of the way all children learn to walk.

The Whole Child Develops

While theories have been formulated to describe growth in the areas of physical, social, emotional, and intellectual development, it is difficult to discuss one apart from the other. Each child grows in all these dimensions at the same time, and in the process of this growth, factors from one area often affect development in other areas.

The way in which language skills are learned illustrates this in a simple way. Studies have shown that the amount of babbling by an infant may be influenced by the amount and kind of response made to the babbles. When persons touch the baby and make "tsking" sounds, the span of time spent in babbling can be prolonged. Since babbling is a prelude to language, this action encourages the baby's early talking attempts. At the same time, this kind of attention is helping the child develop a sense of belonging to a family group. Thus babbling (physical, and intellectual as it relates to language development) and the emergence of a sense of belonging (emotional and social) are both influenced by the touching (physical). Whether the child first says "Daddy bye-bye"or "Mommy bye-bye" depends on the child's ability to form sentences (intellectual) and on the family life-style which determines which parent usually leaves home and which remains behind (social).

Each child acquires language skills according to the same developmental pattern, but the meaning of those words, the emotional overtones they convey, the way in which they are connected, the rate at which they are learned—these are all influenced by the growth taking place in other areas.

This same kind of overlapping occurs in relation to every other aspect of a child's development. It makes research difficult, but it guarantees the uniqueness of every person.

Physical, Social, and Emotional Development

Some of the physical, social, and emotional aspects of a child's development are especially relevant for those who work with children. (Age-group terminology is used in this way: preschool, ages 2-5; early elementary, grades 1-3; and late elementary, grades 4-6.)

Energy Level

It takes a great deal of energy to grow from infancy to adolescence and then to adulthood. Since growth takes place in spurts, the energy level is uneven, too. By the time children reach the preschool years the rapid growth of their earliest years has slowed enough that their energy level is high. They expend this energy in large muscle activities—running, jumping, kicking, throwing—all accompanied by noisemaking. Their attention span, if they are really involved, may be only five to fifteen minutes in length. Often it is much shorter. Their exhaustion is finally evidenced by irritability and restlessness, sometimes even as they persist in the activity. This high level of energy continues into the elementary years. It shows itself not only in physical activity, but in the capacity for great enthusiasm about a project of special interest, or in the ability of late elementary children to argue endlessly!

As the later elementary years arrive, those who are approaching puberty will begin to tire more easily. This is especially noticeable in girls since they mature earlier than boys. It means a great variation in the energy levels between children in any group, and in most cases a variation in energy level for a given child from one day to the next.

> But what if you have asthma or are hooked on drugs or are always tired because your folks yell at each other all night and you can't sleep or because no one is home to get your supper, so you eat French fries at the drive-in most of the time?

Interaction with Significant Persons

Children become persons as they relate to other persons whom they consider to be important. The most significant person in the infant's life is the one who has primary responsibility for its care. Usually this is the mother or father, although it may be an older child in the family, a grandparent, or an employed nursemaid. Soon other members of the family become significant persons, until by the late preschool years neighborhood friends have assumed an important place in the life of the child.

When children enter school the range of important persons quickly enlarges, so that approval is sought not only from adults in the family and neighborhood, but from children their own age as well. This peer approval becomes more and more crucial as they grow older, until by the end of childhood, adult approval, although still needed, is not as sought after as acceptance by one's own peers.

Interaction with other children begins with play. It is through play that children test their skills and their ability to relate to other human beings. At first the play is not *with,* but *in the presence of*, other children, described therefore as *parallel play.* Playing together cannot occur until children are ready to interact with one another on an equal basis, in contrast to the adult-child kind of interaction they have known before. Learning to play cooperatively is one of the tasks of the later preschool years.

Boys and girls play together in the early elementary years. Late elementary boys begin to form gangs, and girls of the same age tend to break into groups of two or three special friends. Although the friendships are off and on, there is a great loyalty to one another when they are on. Heterosexual interest today seems to appear earlier than formerly, although it is difficult to know how much of this is the influence of our culture and how much of it is actual biological change.

Children move from saying "I am you" (identity with the dominant parent figure), to "I am me" (the beginning of self-identity), to "I want to know you" (beginning of the socialization process), to "I like you" or "I don't like you" (development of discrimination and values). Meaningful relationships with the significant persons at each age is essential.

> But what if your parents are divorced and each has remarried, you have brothers and sisters you haven't seen, your grandparents live a thousand miles away, your mother doesn't let you play with the kids in your block because they aren't the "right kind," you are bused to a school three miles in one direction, you go to a church three miles in the opposite direction?

Dependence and Independence

One of the most important tasks of childhood is the move from total dependence on parents toward the ability to care for and make decisions for oneself. It is only when children achieve some degree of autonomy that they are able to assume responsibility for their actions.

Older preschool children have achieved a degree of independence as far as caring for their physical needs is concerned. Toilet and eating habits are generally under control by the time they enter public school kindergarten. Buttons, zippers, shoe laces, bows, and overshoes are in the process of being conquered. This ability makes it possible for children to be more mobile. They can visit friends overnight, attend school, and generally experiment with longer and longer separation from parents.

As children progress through the elementary years they grow increasingly independent in both action and thought, but not without effort and risk. At times it is parents and teachers who hold children back or push them too quickly. At times it is children who are afraid to break away or want to break away all at once. Adults must often seem inconsistent to children at one moment saying, "You'll have to learn to do it yourself. I'm busy!" and at the next moment, "Don't try to do that yourself! You're too little!" This pulling and tugging results in rapid strides toward independence as well as times of slipping back temporarily to the dependence of an earlier age. Both responses are normal and should be expected.

This sense of independence grows throughout the elementary years so that a child moves from pleading, "I can't do it!" to "Please, Mother, I'll do it myself!" and sometimes on to, "Here, I'll do it for you!"

> But what if you are in a wheelchair or are blind or your parents are afraid to let you try new things or you are the baby in the family and no one ever lets you do anything for yourself?

Sense of Right and Wrong

The moral judgment of children is related to their sense of independence, their development as responsible persons, and their desire for approval from the significant persons in their lives. It is these persons who provide them with a large part of their value systems. Children learn that some behavior wins approval and some does not. In their circle of important persons some attitudes are acceptable and some are not. Older preschool children can tell the difference between the acceptable and the unacceptable, especially when it is reinforced by adult approval or disapproval, although they do not always act accordingly.

In the early elementary years children are especially concerned about the question of right and wrong. Fairness emerges as a criterion for judging behavior. Is the punishment fair? Are their friends fair when they play together? Does everyone get an equal share when the snacks are divided? In order to assure that fairness will reign, children of this age become ardent rule-makers. This is a behavior that does not seem to be learned from adults, but is common to children everywhere apparently as a result of solidarity among the children themselves. On occasion the rule-making itself becomes the game and occupies more time than the game for which the rules must be made. Often children will change the rules to suit their own personal advantage, but they do not abandon the concept of rules.

For children in the later elementary years the question of moral judgment begins to shift from What is fair, especially in the behavior of others? to What is right for me to do? It may not always be articulated, and actions may seem to belie the assertion, but in their inner selves children are their own worst critics. When they do not measure up to their own expectations they easily become discouraged.

But what if you always seem to lose when you play by the rules or your friend's mother lets her do things you aren't allowed to do or your father tells you to help him watch for police cars when you are out for a drive or you get scolded when you do something wrong, but no one ever notices when you do something right?

Feelings and Their Expression

Children use their feelings as orchestra members use their instruments, playing them in different ways on different occasions. This makes a live symphony concert more exciting than a recording, and live children more intriguing (and usually more exasperating!) than a book about them.

Emotions are often private, usually elusive, and always changing, so that this aspect of childhood is one of the most difficult to define. Because of the difference in rate of growth and the influence of each child's particular social, mental, and physical growth pattern, there is probably less uniformity in this area than in any of the others. Furthermore, most studies of emotions have dealt with strong motivating emotions such as rage and fear, but not with the more positive affection and joy.

Infant emotions are wholly in response to external factors. Experimentation has shown that by the time children are two years old they respond to their environment with feelings of fear, disgust, anger, excitement, distress, delight, elation, affection, jealousy, and joy. As the child grows older these feelings continue to be exhibited toward persons and things outside the child and, eventually, when directed inward become the basis for the child's own self-concept.

In small children joy is experienced at its height when they are using their whole bodies, being totally involved in running, jumping, and shouting. This can be both the source of joy and the means of its expression. Or joy may come in response to a gift, to a projected favorite activity, or the sight of a friend or a returning parent. Even as children grow older, they feel joy primarily in relation to something pleasant that is happening to them, although because of their growing concept of time they are also able to experience joy as they anticipate future pleasurable events.

Only in older elementary years can children begin to experience joy in relation to abstract ideas. In a service of worship, when children carry banners they themselves have made, banners with words such as God Loves You, God Lives, or Live in Joy, they may find joy in the experience of marching and feeling like a part of the total church community. The making of the banners can be an experience of joy because children are happy when they are making things, especially things that are seen to be of value. But only for a few of the older boys and girls can the abstract phrases on the banners bring joy. Joy for children is a "now" experience. For adults in this worship setting, the experience can be a celebration, a time to say, "See what God has done for me." For children, also, it can be a celebration: "See what I have done—I hope you like it."

The early fears of infancy lessen as children reach the preschool years, although in certain circumstances, loud noises, sudden movements, or strangers can still elicit feelings of fear. In addition, new fears are being learned. Now children may be afraid of animals, the dark, imaginary creatures, being hurt, overly demanding social situations, or long separations from parents.

Through the course of the elementary years, children conquer these fears, one by one, as they begin to feel themselves to be more in control of their environment. Uncertain feelings caused by external circumstances become less significant and are replaced by uncertain feelings about themselves.

Children accept a great deal of love and attention and in return give indications of love, probably in order that the flow of love back to them will not be interrupted. This giving and receiving is the origin of feelings of trust, trust in the dependability of their world. And it is this ability to trust which is basic to later religious development. To paraphrase a familiar Bible verse, "How can you trust God, whom you have not seen, if you cannot trust your world of which you are a part?"

Children are equally capable of negative responses to others, feelings of mistrust, jealousy, and rivalry. For instance, jealousy may be directed toward children who seem to be winning more than their share of adult approval or toward an adult who is enjoying the desired attention of another adult. One preschooler became jealous of her father's doctoral dissertation which took time away from her and, as a result, attacked his typewriter!

As children grow toward adolescence they more and more express feelings of resentment toward adult control, even though the need for adult approval is still strong. In this struggle toward achieving their own identity they sometimes become moody, uncooperative, and even rebellious.

Whereas the emotions of younger children are largely produced by what the world does to them and for them, older children are beginning to respond with feelings about themselves and the way they relate to the world. In the elementary years, self-concept begins to be a more or less conscious developmental task for children. If their earlier years were relatively free from turmoil, they enter this period with a sense of self-assurance and with an eagerness to tackle whatever life brings. But these feelings are often accompanied by doubts and guilt as they slowly move away from dependence on parents and other significant adults. They have learned to discriminate between right and wrong, but sometimes they fail to act accordingly. When they make something and it meets their standards, they are pleased with themselves, but often they fall short of their own expectations. They want to be perfect, so they are easily discouraged. When they are accepted by the significant persons in their lives, whether adults or other children, they experience positive feelings of belonging; on other occasions they feel rejected and therefore undesirable.

So at times children feel good about themselves, at times they dislike themselves, and all the time they are creating a self-image.

> But what if your parents weren't glad to have you, so you never did learn to feel your world and the people in it were trustworthy? What if the kids at school call you bad names and you never feel good about yourself and nobody seems to care how you feel?

Mental Development

Since the Bible contains factual information and abstract concepts, it is important to understand the mental development of children.

Acquiring and Verbalizing Ideas

By the time children are three years of age they have developed an extensive vocabulary and are beginning to construct sentences. Many of the sentences result from their growing curiosity and are in the form of questions: Why? Where? What for? and Who? Much of their speech is in imitation of adults in tone of voice, words, and ideas. One mother, upon meeting her child's kindergarten teacher exclaimed, "Now I know why Mary talks the way she does. She sounds just like you!"

When preschool children venture to express their ideas, they are not always able to discriminate between what has happened in the real world and what is a product of their imaginations.

The words and ideas expressed are related directly to their experiences, so children learn to verbalize most rapidly through participation in a variety of activities. They are more interested in the activity than in its potential for their learning, however.

Children in early elementary years are eager and curious about everything they see. They are beginning to have an interest in the past, especially if it is related to them personally in some way; for example, "This is where we lived when you were a little baby." Primarily, however, they are still present oriented. It is only in the later elementary years that children understand the concept of time—of past, present, and future. It is then that they can begin to understand history and make plans for future events.

Stages in Thinking

It is important to look more closely at the developmental process by which children change experiences into ideas and then learn to use those ideas to meet the demands of their world.

The first step in performing mental tasks is the ability to learn *concepts*. A child may be taught by rote to say, "The ball is round," but the concept *roundness* is not understood until the child is able to apply the word *round* to objects that are not spherical like the ball, but to objects such as wheels, saucers, and cylinders.

The second step in performing mental tasks is the ability to construct *principles*. Rolling and roundness are both concepts. Children show mental growth when they are able to combine the two concepts to form the principle: Round things roll.

The third and most complicated step in mental development is the ability to *combine principles* so as to form more complicated principles and to use these principles in order to solve problems. When the two principles, "Round things roll" and "Friction decreases speed" are combined, a new principle about braking is discovered, and the problem of controlling speed is solved!

All the illustrations so far have dealt with concrete concepts, directly related to objects which can be manipulated. Round objects can be felt. Rolling can be observed. Friction can be applied. Braking can be tested, and the results measured.

Many concepts are not related to objects that can be manipulated. Love, force, faraway, before, spirit, and courage are just a few of the thousands of abstractions we use every day. These abstract concepts cannot be felt, moved, seen, or counted. It is obvious that it takes a higher order of mental development to understand the principle "love conquers force" than to understand "round things roll."

A Swiss psychologist, Jean Piaget, suggests that there

are four major stages in the development of thinking, divided by age approximately into (1) birth to two years; (2) two to seven years; (3) seven to ten or eleven years; and (4) eleven years and over. Piaget asserts that children cannot begin to think in abstract terms until sometime during the third stage, and they cannot actually achieve abstract thinking that is useful and dependable until the last stage. This conclusion is a result of research conducted by Piaget over the last fifty years.

On September 12, 1971, *Newsweek* reported an account of research by Peter Bryant of Oxford University in which he disagrees with Piaget and reports that a three-year-old can be taught to think abstractly. Although no one experiment can discredit the work of half a century, it adds fuel to a controversy that has been raging in the public schools of America for at least the last decade, the results of which are being felt in church education as well.

The Controversy

The controversy related to mental development is not centered around the sequence of steps or stages, but around the question of when a child is able to perform each mental task, at both the concrete and abstract levels, and how this may affect the teaching-learning process. Simply put, the argument is based on the answer to this question: What can children be expected to learn, and how early in their formal educational experience can they be expected to learn it?

As might be anticipated, there have been a variety of responses to this issue from educators whose task it is to make theories visible in classroom procedures. The responses fall into three general categories.

"We have underestimated children's ability to learn."
Those who express this conviction point to the vast
amount of materials children are able to memorize, their
eagerness to learn as expressed through thoughtful questions, their fascination with educational television for
children, the complicated manual tasks they can perform,
and above all, their ability to read at an age far younger
than the traditional six years. As a result of this point of
view, many public schools have introduced reading in
the kindergarten years.

Individualized instruction has been adopted to allow
for the range of mental maturity in a given group of
children. Where public schools have not adopted this
approach, some parents have organized "free schools" or
have supplemented the public school curriculum by
teaching reading at home. Others have enrolled their
children at the age of three in privately operated pre-
schools which promise to teach reading and mathema-
tics.

In the church school this understanding of the mental
ability of children supports a general increase in the
amount of content included in curriculum materials,
especially the amount of Bible material. Most denominational curriculum revisions in the last ten years have been
influenced by the assertion that "we have underestimated
the ability of children to learn."

"Learning includes understanding." While agreeing
generally with the premise that children's abilities have
been underestimated, there are educators who insist that
a word of caution be spoken. That is, the ability to pro-
nounce words or to repeat concepts is not evidence that
real learning has taken place. The important question to

ask is, "Do the children understand what they have read?" Or, "Are they able to apply the concept in another situation?" Public school administrators and teachers who hold this view develop a readiness program to provide a basis on which a reading program can be built. The ability of children to distinguish shapes is determined before they are asked to see the difference between b and p. Care is taken to keep reading vocabulary within the experiences of the child. Where experience is lacking, it may be provided through planned activities. For example, a visit to the airport or a ride on a train may be made prior to reading a story involving various modes of transportation. The concern here is that an emphasis on reading skills is not made at the expense of comprehension.

Religious educators who join in the reminder that "learning includes understanding" point particularly to the abstract nature of important biblical concepts. "Pilots fly planes" is a principle capable of being grasped far earlier in the mental development of a child than the principle "God created the world."

"Growth in all areas of development is important." Some educators are anxious to raise a question about priorities and balance in education. Why is there such an emphasis in the early years on the area of mental growth? Children do not need to know how to read at three or four years of age. This can come later with no loss in future ability to learn. But children do need to achieve adequate emotional and social adjustment. If this is neglected in the early years it will affect negatively their future development, including their ability to acquire reading skills.

A public school with this philosophy specializes in

socialization in the kindergarten, saving the introduction of reading for the first grade. Throughout all the elementary years it will encourage teachers to set individual rather than group goals with the purpose of providing a balanced learning experience for each child. For example, a kindergarten girl who spends most of her time in the book corner will be encouraged to try the block corner for a few minutes each day, while a fifth-grade boy who has interest in baseball only will be encouraged to spend some time in the school library.

In church education this controversy is phrased in a somewhat different way: Why is there such concern that children be able to repeat theological concepts and doctrinal statements? Church education in the early years should develop attitudes about the Bible and the church.

Regardless of the way people respond to this present controversy in education, they all want to know more about the way children develop mentally at each stage so that they can work with this process.

> But what if you are retarded or a slow learner or are gifted and bored or want to be a lawyer but your parents say, "Girls should be secretaries or nurses or mothers"? What if you are supposed to be learning about the Revolutionary War, but you really want to know how to protect yourself from the gang in the next block, or you move several times a year and you can't ever get caught up at school?

Religious Development

Finally we come to religious development only to discover that of all the areas the least research is here, the

76

most inconclusive results, and perhaps the most overlapping with the other areas. Almost all the research has been related to the development of religious concepts, and much of this has centered on the concept of God. There is no evidence in the studies available, however, that refutes Piaget's placement of abstract thinking in the later elementary years.

Jean McClarin Jones has described the preschool period as "the wonder years" ("The Religious Development of Children in Interrelationship with Identity Formation and Conceptual Growth," Boston University School of Theology, Th.D. diss., 1968). Here children attempt to find their identity as distinct objects in a world of many objects and, as a consequence, frequently ask of their parents many *how* and *why* questions. For the moment parents are seen as all-powerful because they have provided their children with all that they have needed. As the children's world expands they transfer this characteristic to other adults until, in imitation of adults, they at last assign to this all-powerful trait the word symbol, *God*. Now there comes a flood of questions about God and the beginning of what we call "religious thinking."

The answers children receive to their religious questions are not intellectually understood by them because they still see God as a person like their mothers and fathers, even though the answers are given in terms of abstract concepts such as love, spirit, or divine. But there is evidence that children do exhibit a "sense" or "feeling" or "experience" of God. It is thought to be present in feelings of awe and wonder, such as those experienced when looking at a beautiful flower, really seeing a sunset for the first time, or watching a newborn baby. Adults explain these mysteries to the children by speaking the name *God*. Whether children eventually come to associate God with love and beauty or with punishment and deprivation depends on their experiences with their world.

Although children in the "wonder years" do not intellectually understand the concepts central to the Christian religion, they can begin to participate in its rituals because of their ability to imitate, and they can begin to use the name of God. Pleasure in this participation comes from the fulfillment of the social need to be a part of what significant adults see to be important and leads to the understanding of themselves as part of the church.

In contrast to the "wonder years" designation, children in the elementary grades are said to be in the "reality-oriented years." They are rooted in the here and now, and the here and now revolves around them as its center. God is one who does things to the child and for the child. Prayers by children in this period stress the personal benefits sought after. All in all, religion for children in the "reality-oriented years" must serve some useful function.

Elementary children ask more specific religious questions than the *how* and *why* queries of earlier years. Now they ask about birth, death, natural disasters, and God's role in all this. Whatever answers are given, whether in direct response or in formal instruction, they are always interpreted by children in terms of their own experiences. They may repeat the same words as those used by the adults, but their concept is never a precise copy of the adult's concept. Misunderstandings occur, therefore, and they tend to persist, leading to other misunderstandings.

As children approach the later elementary years they become more interested in the heritage of the church. They now begin to think abstractly, rather than having to identify each concept with some object in their experience. God no longer needs to be thought of in human form; love is a feeling, not a gift from grandmother, and sorrow is an emotion, not the tears themselves. It is only at this stage that children can begin to understand the doctrines of the church or begin to cautiously express their own faith statements.

But what if your family never attends church and the only time you ever hear the word God is when someone is angry, or you drop out of Sunday school while you still visualize God as a man with a long white beard? Or what if nobody answers your questions, and if they do, you can't understand the answers?

Today's Child: A Stranger

In some ways, today's children are strangers. We have never been where they are. Although their world is changing, we know more about the world than we know about what it is doing to children. But the children are here today, and because we want to guide them in discovering Bible meanings now, we can do these things:

We can become careful observers of the child's world so that we can begin to see and feel how it is different from the one we knew when we were children.

We can use our creative imaginations to feel what it must be like to be a child today.

We can become familiar with those theories about childhood that have already been formulated, while continuing to be alert for new understandings as they become available.

We can avoid the temptation to generalize about children, determining to see each child as a unique individual, with his or her own personality and potential.

How is it possible for children in a rapidly changing world to be confronted by the Bible as an Event, in such a way that they discover in it meaning for their here-and-now lives? The next section describes an appropriate teaching style, four Bible-learning tasks for the childhood years, and teaching methods by which these tasks can be achieved.

1.
Teaching Biblically

Point of View:
To teach the Bible is to talk about life. To talk about life (within the Christian community) is to teach the Bible.

Since the beginning of this century there has been an ongoing debate among Christian educators—teachers, theorists, and curriculum writers. It has revolved around the question of whether teaching should be Bible-centered or life-centered. When asked the question, "What do you teach?" those who hold the first point of view reply, "I teach the Bible"; the second, "I teach children." Compromises have been attempted by offering some alternative centers from which to choose, but these always seem to fall into one camp or the other. At times the lines have been so tightly drawn by each side that any understanding of the other has been impossible. The fact of the matter is, there are some who are closer in thought to people in the other group than they are to some in their own.

The intent of this chapter is to approach each of these points of view as objectively as possible, to show in a visual way the wide range of possible interpretations within each, and finally to propose a basis for teaching the Bible which is neither Bible-centered or life-centered in the traditional sense.

The -Centered Approach

Bible-centered Teaching

Those who describe themselves as Bible-centered teachers place great importance on the text of the Bible and its message. For them the Bible is the place to begin because it is the authoritative source of our Christian faith. An understanding of this approach will be clearer if we look at the way it works itself out in the classroom. Here we discover there are at least four different understandings of what it looks like to be Bible-centered. Each long rectangle represents a session or a unit of study.

There are some teachers who teach *only* the Bible text (Figure 1).

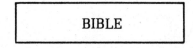

Figure 1.

They emphasize telling and learning Bible stories. While the stories are being told, children may be kept busy coloring Bible pictures with their hands while they listen with their minds. Memorization of Bible verses is encouraged and often aided by the use of Bible drills and rewards.

Most Bible-centered teachers, however, acknowledge to some extent the relationship of the Bible to the life of the child. Some spend a major portion of their time with the Bible material itself, saving for the last few minutes of the session (or the last session of the unit) the question, "How does this relate to our everyday living?" (Figure 2).

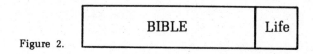
Figure 2.

Others, in order to capture the interest of children, begin the session or unit with a current happening, either in the life of the child or the community (Figure 3).

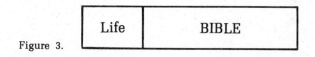
Figure 3.

Then through the eyes of the children's experiences, the major portion of the session is used to help them understand the biblical materials. For example, the story of Moses in the bulrushes might begin with the question, "How many of you have baby brothers or sisters at home?" After acknowledging the verbal responses of the children the teacher would relate their knowledge of babies to the life of Moses.

Still others who call themselves Bible-centered teachers begin the session with the Bible as a basic source (Figure 4). When the meaning of the Bible selections has been established, they devote a sizable amount of time to a comparison of the Bible experience with the contemporary scene, perhaps leading the class to discover some kind of appropriate action it might take. A careful study

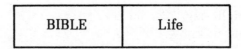

Figure 4.

of the Creation stories, with an emphasis on the continuing creativity of God, might lead a group to a discussion of ecology and a determination to publicize and use the community recycling program.

Teachers who use any of these four teaching plans in their classrooms could describe themselves as "beginning with the Bible" or as being Bible-centered. It is obvious that everyone does not mean the same thing by "Bible-centered."

Life-centered Teaching

Everyone does not mean the same thing by "life-centered," either. Those who describe themselves as life-centered teachers see the experiences of the child to be the place where teaching begins, because Christianity is not a religion in a vacuum, but is centrally concerned with persons. At various times in the history of Christian education this view has been called experience-centered, problem-centered, developmental task-centered, or child-centered. All these are included here in the use of the term "life-centered." Here, too, there are at least four different understandings of what life-centered teaching looks like in the classroom.

There are teachers who reflect on the human situation and who never deal with biblical materials as such (Figure 5).

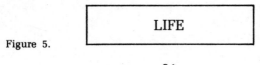

Figure 5.

They might say, "To be a Christian is not to know the Bible, but to know how to live." This quality of life has roots in the Christian tradition, but it is not always necessary to identify its biblical source. Some of the teaching methods used might include discussions of current events, the sharing of experiences, problem-solving, expression of feelings, or participation in activities outside the classroom in order to enlarge the child's world.

Most life-centered teachers to some degree acknowledge the relationship of the life of the child to the Bible. Some of these use the Bible only to validate what has already been learned from experience (Figure 6). For

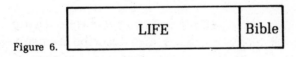

Figure 6.

instance, an entire session or unit might be spent on family relations, teaching a child that to be a responsible member of a family is to be aware of the special concern mothers and fathers have for their children. To summarize the session, the child might be taught to say, "Honor thy father and thy mother."

Others who call themselves life-centered teachers use the Bible as an introduction to the discussion of a life situation (Figure 7). For example, if the story of the good Samaritan is presented at the beginning of the session,

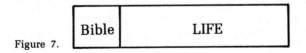

Figure 7.

the major portion of time might then be spent in a consideration of the opportunities children have to be "good Samaritans" at school.

Still others begin with life as the basic motif, using all the time necessary to establish that Christianity is concerned with persons where they are (Figure 8). Then,

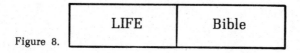

Figure 8.

when this has been established, they devote a sizable amount of time to helping children discover that the Bible contains concerns similar to their own and that it is, therefore, important to be familiar with it.

Persons who follow any of these four general plans could refer to themselves as life-centered teachers, even though there are great differences among them.

An Alternative to a -Centered Approach

There is a similarity between these two different perspectives which is not usually noted. Both have put their emphasis on the *materials* worked with in the teaching-learning process. We are accustomed to thinking of the Bible as containing materials for teaching, so to think of Bible-centered teaching as "materials-centered" is no problem. Less obvious, however, is the fact that for those committed to a life-centered approach, the *experiences of the child* are the basic materials with which the teacher works. The frustration has been the necessity to decide which of these materials would be central in the teaching process. The solution is to abandon neither the materials of the Bible nor of the child's experiences, but to stop trying to organize our teaching around materials at all. Rather, let the teaching style itself be the central concern, leaving the teacher free to use whatever materials are appropriate. And let this style be called *teaching biblically*.

Teaching Biblically

The person who "teaches biblically" lives out in the classroom three basic convictions: (1) It is impossible to separate Bible and life, even should it be desirable to do so; (2) When life experiences are used as the basic materials, they must be interpreted within the context of the Christian community; (3) When Bible materials are used they must be taught experientially. These convictions are not necessarily stated by the teacher, but if they are really convictions, the Bible will come alive for the persons being taught.

Bible/Life —Inseparable

The discussion of the two-centers approach in the previous section was a risky one. If in any way it perpetuates the controversy between Bible- and life-centered teaching, then the risk was too great. This distinction has been a false one from the beginning and is a mind-set which should be eradicated. The fact is, the two are inseparable, for to say "Bible" is to say "life."

The problem with Figures 2, 3, 4, 6, 7, and 8 is that the perpendicular line separates Bible from life. When a person teaches biblically, a session or unit will look more like the rectangle in Figure 9. No matter where the bar is placed in this diagram, each segment still contains both Bible and Life. It cannot be placed in any other way.

Figure 9.

Bible	Life	Bible	Life	Bible
Life	Bible	Life	Bible	Life
Bible	Life	Bible	Life	Bible

The Bible itself verifies this unity in two ways. First, it shows itself in our understanding of the Bible as a written witness to Divine-human encounters. The Bible is not a set of propositions or creeds, but the testimonies of real people who experienced God in their lives. Without this "life dimension" the Bible would not exist.

Second, this unity of Bible and life is evident in our understanding of the Bible as a confronting Event to which we make a response. It is impossible for us to exist anywhere other than in our own life situation, so it is there that the Bible in its completeness confronts us. In this meeting the Bible and our life at that point are experienced as a single event. They are fused together in such a way that they cannot be separated.

If the Bible did not affirm this inseparableness, it would be affirmed by the nature of childhood. Whatever concepts children learn, they do it within the framework of their own experiences. Even if the life situations of children are never acknowledged by the teacher, children must struggle to find a way to fit what they learn about the Bible into their total concept of things.

"Teaching biblically" means not trying to separate Bible/life into two kinds of materials, but teaching in such a way that one will never be thought of without the other.

Interpreting Life-Experience Materials Within the Context of the Christian Community

A teacher need not always deal with the Bible itself to be described as teaching biblically. Because the Bible is a witness to God's encounter with persons in their human situation, this is reason enough to consider life's experiences. While it is not always necessary to find answers to life's problems in specific Bible verses or to discover parallels in the lives of Bible persons, it is important that this examination of personal or social concerns be done within the context of the Christian community. Although this does not limit such teaching to an area within the four walls of the church, it surely means that it will be under the guidance of persons who acknowledge themselves to be within the Christian tradition and who function intentionally, at the request of and answerable to members of the Christian fellowship, usually the church. It also assumes that in previous sessions or units, biblical materials were taught and that this will be true in the future.

If early Christians struggled together to find meaning in their human situation, then it seems consistent with biblical tradition that life concerns today should be worked through with the help of the community of Christians. The church community can serve as a corrective for the interpretations, as a support for those who need encouragement, and as a reminder of our long heritage. It provides the rich resources of the tradition, many of them with their roots in the Bible—the sacraments, the liturgy, and the hymns of the church, for example.

To use today's concerns as materials for teaching, and

to use them within the context of the Christian community, is part of what it means to teach biblically.

Use of Curriculum Materials

Many persons who seek to guide children in a discovery of Bible meanings are church school teachers and parents who have been provided with denominational, interdenominational, or commercial curriculum materials. Some of these materials are labeled Life-centered, some Bible-centered, while others carry no indication of their approach. The label is not the whole story. Some materials are designed so that teaching biblically is the style expected of those who use it. Other materials can easily be adapted to fit this style, once the teacher has a feel for what it means to "teach experientially," which is explained in the next chapter. If the three criteria for teaching biblically are taken seriously, some curriculum materials may be unusable.

Sometimes meaning can be discovered through the experiences of daily living. When it seems desirable to use such experiences for teaching children, they should be used within the context of the Christian community.

At other times meaning is best discovered by a study of the Bible itself. When it seems desirable to use biblical materials for teaching children, the Bible should be taught experientially.

Knowing which approach to use, how to use it, and then using it is called "teaching biblically."

2.
Teaching the Bible Experientially

Point of View:
The Bible should be presented in such a way that children discover meaning in it for their present lives and that the possibility of finding meaning for the future is enhanced.

In addition to death and taxes, one of the things we can be most sure of is the nearly unanimous desire on the part of Christian adults for children to be taught the Bible. However, there is no universal agreement on either the way the Bible should be taught or the reason for teaching it.

Some Other Perspectives

Vague Feeling of "Oughtness"

Many people have never clearly thought through their conviction that it is important for children to know the Bible, except they have a vague feeling that it is desirable. They feel that since it is obviously a religious activity, surely something good will come as a result. Sometimes parents who have declared that religion is no longer important for them personally continue to want for their children a Bible education. Perhaps this indicates a belief

91

that children should have an opportunity to accept or reject the Christian religion for themselves. For some it probably represents a notion that knowledge of the Bible is important in the same way other literature is important—as a part of our cultural heritage. Still others may simply have an uneasy fear and uncertainty about the consequences of not knowing the Bible.

For all these people, what is taught or when it is taught or how it is taught is not as important as *that* it is taught.

Character-Building Theory

The development of moral persons is sometimes seen as the primary reason to engage children in a study of the Bible. Public schools teach children to "do good," and church schools teach them to "be good." The study of the Bible produces Christians, and Christians possess certain personal qualities usually seen to be attributes of good character, and thus good citizenship. Similarly, there are destructive traits and behaviors that Christians, if taught well, do not display—the precise list here depending upon the particular religious group involved.

Selections from the Bible provide moral solutions to the dilemma of how to live as a Christian in the face of each day's temptations and difficulties. The teacher may begin with the Bible and point out a moral, or the class discussion may begin with a real-life problem, whose solution will be evident in an appropriate Bible passage. In either case, the Bible is almost always used to validate the moral values the teacher wants to convey. The importance of the Bible to children is in the value system they take on as a result of its study.

Storehouse/Banking Theory

There are those whose major concern in the use of the Bible with children is that biblical facts and concepts should be learned and "stored" or "banked" for future reference. During the elementary years children seem to have an enormous capacity to learn vast quantities of information with comparative ease. Although they may not understand the words they are learning, this knowledge will serve them well in the future, because the religious thinking that develops in youth and adult years depends on the foundation of information created by this storing and banking process. Furthermore, the ideas learned and stored become part of a body of fact and faith that will be available for times of great crisis.

Those who hold this position specialize in the use of memorization as a teaching method, although they are not limited to this alone. Whatever the method, however, its primary purpose is to promote the retention of biblical facts and concepts. Class discussion is one way to test for this retention.

Readiness Theory

A British educator, Ronald Goldman, has suggested yet another approach which he calls "readiness for religion." His research in the development of religious thinking in childhood and adolescence parallels the stages suggested by Piaget (pages 72-73). This fact, along with his assumption that to be religious one must be capable of abstract thinking, leads him to conclude that children are in a "pre-religious" stage. They do not reach the "religious stage" until the late elementary years. As a consequence, very little of the Bible is taught before children are ten to twelve years of age. To stray from this practice is to run the risk that children will acquire erroneous concepts because of the difficulty of the materials and that they will become bored with too much content given too soon. During preschool and elementary years, Goldman's emphasis is on the religious quality of life's experiences. The Bible may be used to illustrate the meaning of life, never the other way around.

In preschool and elementary years there is a concentration on readiness experiences that prepare children for the abstract religious thinking which will be possible later. Thus, units on sheep and bread, for instance, provide background information that makes later use of biblical stories more understandable.

Like the storehouse theory, Goldman sees the discovery of meaning through Bible study as an event which occurs somewhere in the future. Unlike the storehouse theory, he sees the years of childhood as a preparation for the study of the Bible, not as a time to learn and absorb the biblical materials themselves.

Message of the Bible Theory

The desire to communicate the message in the Bible is seen by some as the only really valid reason for teaching the Bible to children or, for that matter, to anyone. The emphasis is on an understanding of the message itself, rather than on developing morals, giving background information, or aiding in the storage of facts. The content of the message is determined by the theological positions of the curriculum writers and by the way the teachers use and adapt the curriculum materials.

Admittedly, most of the biblical concepts that have

been isolated, organized, and expressed by adults are difficult to understand. Nevertheless, it is possible to make them clear if the experiences of children are used to illustrate the meaning of the Bible message. (This, it should be noted, is exactly the opposite of the "readiness theory.") Here the teacher plans a unit or session by asking first, "What is the biblical concept I want to communicate to the children?" When this has been determined, the concept is taught by choosing activities that correlate with life experiences. Although biblical materials may be used also, an understanding of the concept is what is most important.

Bible Meanings—Now!

No one of these approaches to the use of the Bible with children is wholly adequate. Our primary concern is not that the Bible be meaningful to children at some future time, although the future is important. Neither is our major interest the transfer of a moral code from adult to child, although a rethinking of personal, family, community, or national value systems may be an important result of Bible study. Nor is it our ultimate goal to force a theologically "correct" interpretation of the Bible upon children, although no one wants children to be given an "incorrect" interpretation.

Teaching for Present Meaning

Ever since the Christian community began, it has been convinced that when the Bible becomes real to persons, God is able to speak through it. We have called the Bible a "now" Event through which God confronts us and

95

through which we find meaning for our lives. We want for our children what we want for ourselves. We want children to begin to develop a sense of being special persons who own a special tradition. We want them to begin to find heroes and heroines in the Judeo-Christian tradition as well as in secular history. We want to open the Bible to them so that God can use it to bring meaning to their lives, at whatever level and in whatever ways this is possible. We want children to know the Bible so that they can be confronted by it. We want the Bible to be an important part of the child's "now" world. And we want all of this to happen in their present, not in their future. This sense of immediacy is lacking in the other approaches described.

Is Present Meaning Possible?

But we cannot escape the question that has followed us since the close of the chapter, "A Confronting Event." Can the Bible be for children a confronting Event? There are three views, when seen in relation to one another, that support an affirmative answer to that question.

1. *The Bible is experience.* If the Bible is seen only as a collection of abstract religious concepts, and if to be Christian is to affirm these abstractions, it is useless to talk about the Bible and the religious life of children. We have already noted that children are unable to deal with such abstractions until at least the older elementary years. The solution would be to follow Goldman's proposal that in their early elementary years we help children get ready to be religious when they are ten or twelve years old.

But if we believe that the Bible and life cannot be

separated and understand the Bible as a witness to how God has confronted and can continue to confront persons in their real-life situations, we realize we are not dealing with a book of abstract concepts, but with reports of human experience. The Bible is a "living book" that speaks about the whole human situation and requires that we bring to the study of it all the abilities we possess, not just our ability to think abstractly.

2. *Children have experienced.* Children do not come empty to their encounter with the Bible. They bring a vast reservoir of past experiences, so that when children meet the Bible, it is a meeting of experience with experience. As teachers better understand the development of children, and as they come to see the changing world through the eyes of children, they learn how to use the experiences children bring to the teaching-learning process.

It should never be forgotten that part of the child's world is the presence in it of the Christian community. Although many factors affect religious development, the way children think, their emotional and social lives, and even their view of themselves is influenced by their identity as a member of a particular religious community. And the past experiences with that community, along with all of their other experiences, are the lenses through which they view all the events in their lives.

3. *Children can experience.* If what we have said about children is true, it is unreasonable to expect them to find and express meanings by the use of abstract thinking and wordings. However, it is not unreasonable to expect them to find and express meanings with the abilities they do possess. Rather than regret the absence of one kind of ability, we rejoice and build on the presence of others.

—*Children can feel emotions.* They feel joy, anger, fear, and loneliness, for example. They can feel a sense of belonging or a sense of awe and wonder. They can express their feelings through drama, art, dance, and music—and sometimes through words. When other people exhibit strong feelings, they often experience the same emotions. The many aspects of the problem of suffering unfolded in the story of Job cannot be intellectually understood, but children know how it feels to be judged in a way that seems unfair. They can know what it is like to have friends make fun of them for something they cannot help. They may not understand the cry of a nation, "O God, why dost Thou cast us off for ever?" (Psalm 74:1), but they can imagine what it would be like to come home alone to a locked and empty house.

—*Children are curious.* Once they get hold of a question, they will not let it go. They may not understand the theological differences in the two creation stories in Genesis, but they want to know how the world began. And they like to know that other people have asked the same question and found answers that satisfied them.

—*Children can manipulate things.* Through the use of elementary research tools and techniques, children are able to discover answers to some of their own questions. They can find answers on cassette tapes, in filmstrips, in dictionaries, in concordances, and in the Bible.

—*Children can identify with others.* They can identify with living persons and with persons in fiction and in history. In the important adults of the children's own lives they can see themselves when they are older. As they identify with these adults the children tend to take on the adults' values. By the time children are in kindergarten their circle of important persons has extended to include those beyond their immediate families so that church school teachers may become influences. When they do, teachers have an opportunity through their own attitudes to teach attitudes toward the Bible.

Those who guide children in the discovery of Bible meanings can build on all of these abilities. In the intentional learning experiences provided by the Christian community, they can totally involve children by giving them opportunities to use all their senses, their bodies, their curiosities, their imaginations, their emotions, as well as their emerging abilities to think in abstract terms.

When children experience the Bible, they discover meaning in their own experiences because the Bible deals with human concerns. It speaks to the reality within each child, thus becoming a "now" Event.

Teaching for Future Meaning

Meaning for the present, as important as this is, cannot be the only consideration, because the child's future will be the youth's present.

In the childhood years it is not possible, or even desirable, to provide a complete Bible education. There are youth and adult years ahead in which meaning must continue to unfold. If the Bible is presented in the right way there will be no barriers erected in childhood that will tend to fix meaning at a child's level, limiting future understandings. Nor will there be fostered the notion that "I've learned it all" so no further Bible study is necessary.

To teach for present meanings by building on the nature of the Bible as experience and the nature of the child as one who lives and grows in a sea of experiences—and to keep the Bible open for future interpretations—is what it means to teach the Bible experientially, and therefore part of what it means to teach biblically.

Teaching experientially means finding ways to teach so that the Bible becomes as exciting an Event as yesterday's birthday party or tomorrow's space adventure. It means presenting the Bible in such a way that it becomes an exciting Event that is happening to children now, rather than a dull recital of things that happened a long time ago. It means helping children experience the Bible as a living book that holds the possibility of becoming for them a confronting Event. Children taught in this way will feel with the Bible people rather than be told how they felt. They will find Bible persons with whom to identify. They will come to feel that the Bible is their book. And slowly but surely they will absorb the Judeo-Christian tradition and make it their own.

3.
Teaching the Bible Purposefully

Our exploration for new directions is almost at an end. Its starting point was the Bible itself, which invites us to explore it and experience it as a confronting Event and offers the possibility that through this experience meaningful Divine-human dialogue can take place.

Our exploration then moved to an attempt to understand the nature of childhood in a changing world, where we discovered that children bring much more to their encounter with the Bible than their limited mental abilities.

Next our exploration led us to the necessity of finding an approach to teaching the Bible that did not depend on an artificial separation of Bible and life. This was accomplished by shifting from an emphasis on the materials of teaching—whether Bible or experience—to an emphasis on a teaching style we called teaching biblically and which required that the Bible be taught experientially.

In this chapter we think about the question of what is to be taught. What do we hope for children to know, to feel, to be able to do by the time they reach adolescence, as far as the Bible is concerned? What are the Bible-learning tasks of childhood?

As adult Christians, we feel a need for at least four

kinds of Bible knowledge. First, we want to know the *content* of the Bible. Second, we want to know the *meaning* of the Bible. Third, we want to know about the *background* of the Bible. Fourth, we want to be able to *find our way* in the Bible.

The development of this knowledge can begin in childhood. It is broadened and deepened in the youth years. And it continues as Bible-learning tasks for growing Christians through all of life.

In childhood there is a special flavor associated with each of these Bible-learning tasks. The content of the Bible is *experienced*. The meaning of the Bible is *discovered and expressed*. The background of the Bible is *absorbed*. And skills in the use of the Bible are *acquired*.

Experiencing Bible Content

The Bible does not become an Event for children if teachers attempt to transfer ideas from their minds to the minds of the children. Concepts arise out of experience. If children actually experience the Bible, it will be so vivid that it will become a part of their lives now. This does not mean that they will see Bible events as current history, but that their association with the Bible will be a vital part of their real world. They will feel it, participate in it, handle it, own it. They will identify with the Bible characters. They will name their dogs and dolls Moses, Ezekiel, Mary, or Priscilla. They will hold imaginary conversations with Jesus or Paul or Abraham. They will turn the back yard or the alley or the barn into the temple, the stable, or Noah's ark. The Bible will not be something that belongs only to the past or the church or the teacher, but once they really experience it, it will belong to them—the children.

All the teaching methods known that can bring the Bible to life will be used. Since Bible stories will account for the greatest share of biblical materials used with children, the ability to tell stories will be important. But we will not depend on words alone.

We will use art to accompany the stories—the masterpieces, contemporary art, art from other countries. We will use music—the psalms accompanied by children playing their rhythm instruments, hymns from the church's hymnal, children's songs, music to dance to. We will use drama—stories to pantomime, plays to read aloud, puppets through which to act, scripts to write and produce. We will use audio-visual materials as long as they are fast moving, dramatic, involving, and concerned with story line rather than facts. They can be projected pictures accompanied by a sound track or stories recorded on records or cassette tapes.

Sometimes we will plan activities that prepare children to enter into the spirit and feelings of the Bible story. Children can search the classroom for a well-hidden dime and then hear the story of the Lost Coin. They can paint a picture of how it feels to be lost—and found—and then hear the story of the Lost Sheep. They can be led through creative drama in an experience of what it is like to be hot and tired and lost in a desert and then hear the story of the Exodus. They can observe a baptism in the sanctuary and then hear the story of Jesus' baptism by John.

We will use some parts of the Bible that are not stories if they can be made real to children. Children can become familiar with the Ten Commandments, not as a moral code, but as part of a dramatic episode in the life of Moses. Children can use the Lord's Prayer, not as something to be learned by rote because it is there, but as a result of hearing it in worship experiences—beside their parents and other adults in the sanctuary and with their peers in the classroom.

There are some things we will not do. We will not suggest that retention of facts is the reason for telling Bible stories by requesting a playback of facts at the end of each story, or at the next session of the class. We will not append a moral to every story or wrap it up with, "This means that" statements. We will not present Bible stories in a dull manner or imply they are dull by saying, "After we have had our Bible story then you can paste, color, or go outside and play—that is, have fun."

Only if Bible materials are presented so that they touch some respondent chord in the child will they have meaning.

Only if the Bible has meaning now will children look forward with expectation to the discovery of Bible meanings in the future.

Discovering and Expressing Bible Meanings

To say that Bible meanings are discovered is to say something special about the methods used to teach children the Bible. A uniquely shaped seashell, found after a search on a hot and windy beach and in the company of favorite people, is kept in a treasure box for a lifetime. A seashell dangling at the end of a key chain purchased at the discount store or given by a casual acquaintance is soon discarded.

The significant meanings that come as a result of the

interaction of children with the Bible are not those transferred from teacher to child, but those that surface as personal discoveries. They may or may not be the same ones found in the story by the teacher. But they belong to the child.

To speak of children discovering meanings in the Bible is not necessarily to speak of earthshaking insights that will forever change their lives. But it is to acknowledge that whenever children are really involved in an experience they will attach importance to it. Their understanding may seem right, or it may be judged by us to be wrong, but in either case it is their understanding. It is a mistake to assume that the meanings discovered will be, or ought to be, crystal clear to the child. It is equally wrong to assume that every Bible passage has only one correct meaning. There are no final meanings. It is always possible to receive new insights, and good teaching keeps the doors open that will lead to further understanding.

After children have experienced something in the Bible, there are four levels at which they can begin to discover meanings. The first is, "What does it mean to me right now—as a child?" The second, "What does it mean to you—my teacher, parent, or adult friend?" The third, "What did it mean to them—the original storytellers and listeners?" And fourth, "What does it mean to us as members of the Christian church in the world today?"

What Does It Mean to Me?

The immediate response to any exciting event is at the personal meaning level. If the Bible is really an Event which is made to live, the experience will produce in children a wide range of possible meanings. Adults can aid the exploration and discovery of "What does it mean to me?" in three ways:

First, with children of all ages by being alert to hear meanings when they are expressed spontaneously. Such expression is our best clue as to how children are understanding the Bible.

Second, with early and older elementary children by asking questions and encouraging responses. Often this can be in a conversation or discussion group. A variety of questions can be asked:

> What does the story mean to you?
> What did the story say?
> What did you like about the story?
> Did it remind you of anything?
> Whom did you like best? Why?
> If you had been David, what would you have done?
> What did you think about the way the story ended?
> How else might it have ended?

Sometimes the response can be in written form. When asked to vote for the person she liked best in the story of the prodigal son, one child marked the ballot for the father and explained, "Because he understood that the boy had to go." Another voted for the son who stayed home as the character most disliked because "he was a spoiled brat!" Sometimes the meaning can be expressed in a poem or a story or a prayer.

At other times the response will include nonverbal forms. The teacher can suggest:

> Paint a picture about the story.
> Fingerpaint how the story made you feel.

Show how you think Moses felt by the way you
stand or move around the room.

Act out the story using puppets.

And during these activities the teacher can be alert for
clues that reveal how children have heard and are interpreting the biblical material.

Third, with children of all ages by allowing and accepting the meaning responses that are made. If we ask a
guest in our home, "How is the temperature in the house
for you?" and the guest responds honestly, the answer
cannot be wrong. If he or she answers, "I am a little
chilly" although the thermometer indicates eighty degrees, we cannot validly say "You are wrong. You aren't
chilly." We can say that we ourselves are not chilly; we
can show our guest the thermometer; we can offer articles
that cite sixty-eight degrees as the ideal house temperature. But in no way can we deny the fact that our guest
feels chilly. In fact, if we were not going to accept the
answer given, the question should never have been
asked.

Similarly, if children are asked what a Bible story
means to them, the answer cannot be wrong. It may not
match our own understanding or that of the Bible commentaries we have consulted. It may not seem adequate
to us, but it is not wrong. If that is what the child under-
stands, then that is what it means.

As the teacher asks the question and accepts the response, children begin to learn an important lesson: "The
Bible is more than stories. It is a book that has meaning
for the adults in my life, and they think it can have
meaning for me, too." And when the responses of children are accepted in good faith, they begin to learn a

second lesson which is: "I can be a Bible interpreter, too."

There are some things we should not do. We can avoid questions that require predetermined answers. This practice results eventually in hypocrisy on the part of children because they tell us what they think we want to hear. When this happens, teachers and parents receive wrong data from the children.

We can avoid interpreting aloud a child's art work or other nonverbal responses. And we can avoid saying that children's meanings are wrong.

But no conscientious teacher will want to leave the process at this point for very long. Therefore, the teacher will move to the next meaning level where the child asks, "Teacher, what does this Bible story mean to you?"

What Does It Mean to You?

To request and accept the meanings of children and to withhold our own is not only unfair, but it is to miss one of the most important teaching opportunities we have. In the same spirit with which we accepted the child's meaning response, we can now share our own. We do not do it to correct a wrong idea or to establish a standard by which children can evaluate their understandings, but we do it because we recognize the child as a member of the Christian community with whom we want to share our faith.

Our responses to the child's meaning statements may take varied forms. If the child expresses our own idea we might respond with, "I think that, too. I wonder if there are boys and girls or teachers here who have a different idea to share with us?" If a child expresses a concept unlike our own, we can acknowledge the difference. We might respond, "That's a new idea! I've never thought about it like that before. To me it means . . ." Or, "I used to think that, too. Now I think . . ." When children are led to respond to biblical materials in nonverbal ways, such as drawing or using puppets, it is helpful if teachers have participated in these activities, also. This makes it possible for adults to share with children at both the verbal and nonverbal levels.

As a result of this mutual sharing, children may learn several things: "The important people in my life and I share something important. We both find meaning in the Bible." Or, "Even adults are still discovering new meanings in the Bible." Or, "It will be all right to change my mind later on."

Helping children find Bible meanings does not stop with the personal meanings of children and their teachers.

What Did It Mean to Them?

Part of our teaching task is to help children know that the Bible and its stories had meaning for people a long time ago, too. With some early elementary children and with older elementary children we can raise the question, "I wonder what this story meant to the very first people who ever heard it?" or "I wonder why people thought this story was so important that they wrote it down?"

Here again the most important point is not to teach the right answer, although teachers will want to consult Bible commentaries to discover what answers may be given there. The important thing is to help children realize that the Bible did not just happen, that real people told the stories because they had found meaning in the

109

events in the stories, that there was purpose in the minds of those who retold and wrote down the stories, that real people heard the stories and from the beginning real people have found meaning in them. In this way the dialogue is broadened from the child and you (the adult), to include them (the first storytellers and listeners).

What Does It Mean to Us?

"Us" here refers to the Christian church at this particular time in history. Older elementary boys and girls can begin to think about the relationship between our biblical heritage and the mission of the church in the world today. What does a particular story mean if taken seriously by the Christian community? In response we do not state a final answer, but we share our insights with one another.

By the time children reach this level of meaning discovery, an important thing has happened. The understanding of meaning has gone from a distinctly personal one that is based in present experience, to a dialogue of meaning with contemporary adult Christians, to a dialogue with the Bible writers in the past, and now returns to the present with a wider view of the whole world today. In the process the child's understanding of the Bible has expanded so that it is seen not only in individual terms, but in terms of "me" in relation to other Christians.

A movement through these four levels of meaning during the elementary years paves the way for exploration of a fifth level of meaning in adolescence: "What has the Bible meant to us (the church) historically?" Here the complicated study of heresies, councils, theological systems, and creeds can be begun with the recognition that the effort to find and express Bible meanings continues into adult life.

Absorbing Bible Backgrounds

"Bible backgrounds" has become a catch-all category. Here is contained information about the *land* of the Bible, including topography, climate, locations of cities and villages; *customs,* including dress, family life, village life, and religious life; *literary forms,* including oral tradition, legend, myth, miracles, proverbs, parables, stories, laws, prophecies, songs, letters, poetry, speeches, sermons, and history; the *making of the Bible,* including writing the oral tradition, canonization, translations, and revisions. To introduce Bible stories to children as if these stories were unrelated to geography, customs, origins, literary forms, and Bible development would not be honest.

The primary Bible-learning tasks of childhood are to experience the content of the Bible and to discover meanings. In the process of aiding these two important tasks, we can accomplish a third almost unnoticed. Bible background information can be woven into the stories as they are told much as one opens an important conversation today with the words, "Yesterday I met Joe Jones just outside the post office, and he said . . ." The word *absorb* describes the most appropriate method of teaching Bible backgrounds.

Here are illustrations of how one storyteller encourages the absorption of Bible background facts. The selections are from the *Young Readers Book of Bible Stories* by Helen Doss (Nashville: Abingdon Press, 1967).

The Land

In telling the story of "The Sower and the Seed" the mood is set:

> One cool winter day Jesus left his house in Capernaum. He walked through the crowded streets of the city and then westward along the shore of Lake Galilee, where a great plain pushed back the crowding hills (p. 276).

Children can find Capernaum and Galilee on the map, if they wish. The precise location is not as important as the visual image created in imagination.

Religious Customs

In the story of the prodigal son (or "The Loving Father"), an explanation such as this makes the story even more dramatic:

> To a Jew, the pig was not only the most despised animal he could think of, but was religiously "unclean." Anyone who worked with pigs became contaminated, ritually unfit to worship or associate with other Jews (p. 269).

Literary Forms

The oral tradition as the early form of many Bible stories is absorbed when a story begins,

112

> After supper the families would gather around the campfire as the evening stars began to brighten. ... Everyone would listen as a grandfather or one of the elders of the clan retold some treasured tale that had been passed along from one storyteller to another (p. 11).

The literary form might be indicated by naming it,

> So Jesus replied by telling this parable (p. 271),

or by indicating when using the "Song of Solomon,"

> As the wedding guests were eating, two young singers began to chant the verses of a marriage song (p. 204),

or by explaining,

> Some time after his first missionary trip with Barnabas, Paul began to hear disturbing reports from some of his newly established Christian churches. ... So the apostle wrote a careful letter to the Galatians (p. 343).

The Making of the Bible

When we begin a story from Mark by, "This is a story from the very first Gospel ever written," children come to understand that the Bible was not written all at one time.

When we open a story from Isaiah by saying, "This story is from a book that was written by several different people," children begin to understand something about the problem of authorship. This adds to the growing realization that Bible writers are real people.

When a story read directly from the Bible is preceded by statements such as, "This is the way the story is told in The New English Bible," or "This is from the translation ordered by James, the King of England, over three hundred fifty years ago," children become aware that the Bible is still the Bible, even in different revisions and translations.

When Bible backgrounds are presented in these ways, children understand early that there is much to know about what is in the Bible and how it came to be and knowing this makes it even more exciting and full of meaning.

Acquiring Bible Skills

By the time most children complete their elementary years they should be able to find Bible references, use a simple concordance and a child's Bible dictionary, and at least be aware of the existence of commentaries.

One effective teaching method is to let children see the teachers using such tools. As children become involved with a particular story or passage, the casual suggestion to look it up can send some to the Bible. We should be alert to provide such encouragement and ready to help each child learn the skills at the moment they are needed. When children show an interest in acquiring Bible skills, they may be given the programmed instruction guide, *Finding Your Way Through the Bible,* by Paul B. and Mary Carolyn Maves. A chart or three-dimensional model of the Bible as a library can help children locate the books of the Bible in relation to one another.

Of course, it is possible to teach children Bible skills simply as skills, but this would seem to be a poor use of time. Bible drills are often in the form of games. The problem is, they become win/lose exercises, and the same children usually lose. How rapidly a reference is found is not nearly as important as *that* it is found. Skill training should be on an individual basis, as the need arises, not as a competition. To never find the reference first might cause many children to conclude that to try to use the Bible is discouraging business.

What Children Will Learn

Children who have been helped to experience Bible content, discover and express Bible meanings, absorb Bible backgrounds, and acquire Bible skills will enter adolescence with a wide knowledge of Bible facts and content, not because this was the primary goal, but as a welcome by-product. Many people would be satisfied with this as the only result of Bible study with children.

As desirable as this may be, it is not good enough. Much more should be achieved during childhood years than merely acquiring Bible knowledge. Here are some of the results that might be anticipated:

1. The Bible will be an Event in the lives of children because, in addition to hearing about it, they have actually experienced it. They have been Joseph in the well and Daniel in the lion's den; they can imagine how Moses felt when God gave him the Ten Commandments; they have sat and listened to Jesus, and they have felt bewilderment at the fact that he had enemies; they have been shipwrecked with Paul; they have seen the lame man

walk; they have been Peter and Thomas and Judas and Mary. They feel at home with the Bible.

2. Children will not be trapped by their early, immature concepts of the Bible, God, and Jesus because from the very beginning they have learned that the Bible has unlimited meanings, and as people grow and have new experiences the Bible becomes the source of new and deeper insights. Ideas often change, and that is all right. The doubts and questions of adolescence will not be increased by a rigid certainty of childhood, because throughout childhood boys and girls have been encouraged to discover answers for themselves and are comfortable with the knowledge that among Christians there are many different interpretations of the Bible.

3. Children will be able to talk about their Christian faith because adults have taken time to talk with them about the Bible at that meaning level.

4. Children will begin to see themselves as part of the long line of biblical interpreters which began with the Bible writers.

5. Children will begin to recognize that through the Bible God confronts not only individuals but the church itself, of which they are a part.

6. When the subject of literary forms in the Bible is introduced in junior high, senior high, or college, it will all sound familiar and natural, although the young person may not realize why. The information they unconsciously absorbed in their elementary years will provide a basis for serious Bible study at this later age.

7. Children will see the Bible as a book to be studied as well as experienced and will be acquainted with basic

tools of biblical research: the Bible, commentaries, concordances, dictionaries, and atlases.

Our exploration is at an end—for the moment. We want children to be confronted by the Bible as an Event. This can happen if we understand the potential of children, if we teach the Bible experientially, and if we help children accomplish the Bible-learning tasks of childhood.

How would this approach to the Bible and children look if put into practice? In the next section these four Bible-learning tasks are discussed in relation to three different models: (1) The traditional Group/Team Teaching approach; (2) Learning Centers, and (3) Intergenerational groups.

1.
Discovery Through Group/Team Teaching

Sally Scott, Bob Mitchell, and Donna Washington stood by the piano in the fifth grade room at First Church, checking with one another on the plans for the morning. When the children began to arrive they joined them and encouraged them to look at the pictures posted on the walls around the room.

"See if you can figure out what our new unit of study is going to be about!"

In a few minutes Sally called the children to the circle of chairs. Although they told about pictures of people, flowers, stars and planets, animals, mountains, rockets, cars, bicycles, and Bibles, they were puzzled about the unit theme.

Finally Rick blurted out, "It just looks to me like we're going to talk about everything in the whole world!"

Bob Mitchell laughed and said, "Rick, you're right! That's just what we are going to do—think together about God's whole world." Turning to the group Bob asked, "What would you like to find out about God and his world?"

Donna Washington went to the blackboard and began to record the children's questions.

A visitor, leaving the room at this point, had already seen enough to accurately observe, "This class is using the 'group/team teaching' model."

Group/Team Teaching Is . . .

The way a group of teachers and learners develop their goals, use their room, schedule their time, and choose their learning activities results in an educational plan that is called a *model*.

In this brief, ten-minute glimpse into a church school class, five characteristics of the group/team teaching model are apparent.

First, more than one teacher is responsible for guiding the session. Because they work cooperatively they are known as the *teaching team*. They have planned together prior to the session, and during the class itself they work together, supplementing and supporting one another.

Teaching teams can organize themselves in a variety of ways. In some teams one teacher takes major responsibility and is assisted by several helpers. Other times team members perform tasks according to their own particular talents or interests. In still other situations a group of teachers will share leadership equally, working out specific roles in terms of each session's needs. The common ingredient is the presence of two or more teachers who have planned together and who then share teaching tasks during the session.

Second, class members are grouped according to age or grade level. In the illustration at the beginning of this chapter the class is composed of boys and girls from one grade only. Other class groups might include children from two or three grades. In fact, group/team teaching is not limited to children, but is effective with youth and adult groups as well.

Third, teaching plans are based on unit themes which continue for more than one session—usually at least three or four—depending on the nature of the theme and the age of the group members. A theme such as "God's Whole World" might be divided into smaller sub-units. For each theme there are goals that guide teachers as they plan and evaluate.

Fourth, the presence of a teaching team makes it possible to involve children in a variety of activities. Some of these will be individual, as when each child looked at the picture display. Others will be total group activities, such as the discussion about the pictures, the listing of questions they wanted answered, or the singing and worship that will take place later in the session. Other activities will be in small groups. If we look in on the class next week we might see one group of children making a star map for use by astronauts, while another is making a mural showing the creation stories in the first chapters of Genesis. A third group might be preparing a list of questions about science and religion to ask the minister and the high school science teacher on the fifth grade TV talk show, "Meet the Kids."

These four characteristics describe *team teaching*, which can be done apart from group/team teaching. Team teaching has been the organizational and teaching style followed by curriculum writers of major denominations for at least a generation.

Team teaching becomes "group" or "group/team teaching" when a new dimension is added. It is when as far as they are able, the students are involved in the planning process, also. The team of Sally, Bob, and Donna planned together in advance, but part of their planning was the expectation that in the first session the children would help set the agenda for the remaining sessions by listing their questions about God and his world.

The traditional team teaching sometimes suggests that it is the teachers who should know and the children who should learn. In group/team teaching, children who are learners can also be planners, and teachers who are planners can also be learners. Therefore, the fifth characteristic of group/team teaching is that although teachers and students have their own unique roles, they are co-planners and co-learners.

Although group/team teaching has distinct advantages, especially when a class is large, many of the methods described in this chapter can be used in the one-teacher class setting. A resourceful leader can offer activity options by having more than one activity available and letting the class choose which it will do or making plans so that only one of the activities will require close adult supervision. The leader of a single-teacher class can involve the children in setting goals and planning how to reach them and in this way make it truly group teaching even without benefit of a teaching team.

Understandings on Which Group/Team Teaching Builds

The Bible witnesses to the fact that God made himself known to ancient peoples through the events of their community life. Part of the group/team teaching approach is the awareness that the group of children and adults are potentially a community whose experiences together provide a setting for the God/human encounter.

Group/team teaching is consistent with what we know about the nature of childhood.

1. Children need relationships that are more than casual with children and adults other than those in their own families. The group experience in the church school class provides an opportunity for these relationships to develop.
2. Children of different ages have different interests and abilities. The graded approach to grouping children takes account of these differences.
3. Children are able to work together cooperatively, creating rules as needed. When teachers build on this ability, they turn team teaching into group teaching.
4. Children learn as they work with one another under the guidance of the teaching team.

Group/Team Teaching and the Bible-Learning Tasks

The teaching model with which the Bible is introduced to children is important, but the central part of the process is in the session or unit plan itself. The teaching team consciously seeks to help children with the four Bible-learning tasks:

—experiencing the Bible content
—discovering and expressing Bible meanings at four different levels
—absorbing Bible backgrounds
—acquiring Bible skills

Throughout the rest of this book these code words will be used to indicate specific Bible-learning tasks:

content—experience Bible content

meaning-me—discover and express meaning for me (the child)

meaning-you—discover and express meaning for you (the other)

meaning-them—discover and express meaning for them (those who first told or heard the Bible narratives)

meaning-us—discover and express meaning for us (the church today)

backgrounds—absorb Bible backgrounds

skills—acquire Bible skills

The following session outline illustrates how a session can be planned using the Bible-learning tasks as guidelines. The age and interests of the group will determine the amount of time spent on each part of the session.

A Session Outline: "The Lost Sheep"

Bible References: Ezekiel 34:12; Matthew 18:10-14; Luke 15:3-7

As Children Arrive: Simple puzzles have been placed on tables around the room. Teachers encourage children to join a group. One piece from each puzzle has been removed and is hidden somewhere in the room. As children make this discovery they are urged to search for the lost piece.

Rules

(1) Any piece that is found but does not fit the puzzle must be returned to its hiding place. (2) The hiding place must not be revealed to another group.

(3) When the puzzle is completed, children join the teaching team in the circle.

Conversation: Let children talk about the "game" and how they felt when they could not find the lost puzzle piece.

Story: Tell the story of the lost sheep in a dramatic way. Introduce it with a statement about parables and why Jesus used them (backgrounds). Aid the storytelling with the use of a picture or a series of pictures (content).

Variation 1. The teaching team dramatizes the story for the class (content).

Variation 2. The entire class dramatizes the story—including teachers—with one person acting as the "lost sheep" who must be found (content).

Conversation: "How does this story make you feel?" Help children compare how they felt about the lost puzzle piece with how they feel about the "lost sheep." Do not force likenesses or differences. Accept! (meaning-me).

Creative Activities: "Sometimes talking isn't the best way to say something important." Let children choose one of the following activities with which to further express the meaning of the story for them (meaning-me).

Use rhythm instruments or write a song about the story.

Paint a picture.

Write a poem.

Members of the team will be prepared to guide these activities. If all children choose to paint, let them! Teachers should participate in these activities, too.

Conversation: Let the children share what they have done during the activity period. Listen to the "meaning" comments (meaning-me). Respond in encouraging, accepting ways.

One way teachers can respond is to share their own understandings (meaning-you).

"I wonder why Jesus told this parable?" (backgrounds).

"I wonder what the people who first heard it thought it meant?" (meaning-them).

"I wonder why people told the story over and over again until it was finally written down—at two different places in the Bible!" (meaning-them; backgrounds).

(Teachers will know from their reading of a Bible commentary that each account was told for a different reason. Luke wanted to say that God is joyful when a sinner repents. Matthew wanted to remind the leaders of the church that they should be concerned about the new and immature believers. The story was probably told originally to defend Jesus against those who criticized him when he seemed too interested in outcasts and sinners) (meaning-them; backgrounds).

"Suppose someone walked in right now and told us the story of the lost sheep and said, 'This is especially for the children and teachers in this class!' What do you think they might mean?" (meaning-us).

Teachers will accept the speculations offered by the children; they will not push for comments if children are not ready to think in these abstract terms.

Preparation for Closing: While some children are cleaning paints and others are choosing pictures of Jesus as a shepherd for the worship center, those who wish may find the two accounts of the story in the Bible (skills). These may be read during the closing worship moments.

Worship: Informal moments during which teachers and children gather together the threads of the session. Results of the creative activities are used as parts of the worship service—the poetry written, the pictures painted, the song composed, and the Bible references found (content).

More Bible-Learning Task Activities

Each Bible-learning task does not have a set of activities that guarantees learning. While doing one activity a child may be learning several things at the same time. For convenience, however, the activities suggested below are grouped according to one of their primary uses. These are a few of the ways to open the Bible to children.

To Experience Content

The best ways to experience the content of the Bible (aside from hearing the stories while sitting on the shore of the Sea of Galilee!) are:

1. Excellent storytelling (also *backgrounds*)
2. Creative drama (also *backgrounds*)

One of the values of the group/team teaching model is that by being part of a group, children experience more than they would otherwise. Being held spellbound through storytelling or creative drama when one is part of a group may leave a more lasting impression than when one hears or engages in dramatic play alone. There is a danger here. Sometimes spellbinders are tempted to control the group's responses or manipulate the group's feelings. The integrity of each child's expression of personal meaning must be honored.

3. Well-produced and well-directed films (also *backgrounds*)

To help children feel the mood of certain parts of the Bible, especially the Psalms, it is effective to guide children in the experience of

4. Choral reading

Try this combination of activities. Let older elementary children gather around the lectern or pulpit while looking at the Bible there. Listen to a dramatic recording or ask a good storyteller to narrate some of the history of the Bible as a book, as if the Bible itself were speaking. Tell about the people who were punished for translating it, about the Bible that was chained, about the importance of the invention of printing. Ask the minister to read the Twenty-Third Psalm while the children join in saying the words (also *meaning-you, -us; backgrounds*).

To Discover and Express Meaning for Me

The group/team teaching model provides a community in which meanings can be explored. The more that children feel their sincere efforts to express their ideas are accepted, the more they are willing to share. It is important to encourage all the children to express themselves so that the most talkative and persistent are not the only ones heard.

Here are some ways to help a group of children express the personal meanings the Bible has for them:

1. Guide the group in the creation of a litany, using a Bible verse, perhaps from the Psalms, as a recurring responsive phrase (also *content*).

2. Tell the story of Moses and the Exodus. Then encourage children to show how the people must have felt when they finally escaped. Provide clay, fingerpaints, poster paints, rhythm instruments, or wire (also *content*).

3. Tell the story of the prodigal son (Luke 15:32). Simulate a city election. Prepare ballots. Ask each child to go to a "booth" and vote.

Ballot

The person in the story I liked least: (check one)

_____the father

_____the older son

_____the boy who left home

Why? _____

The person in the story I liked most: (check one)

_____the father

_____the older son

_____the boy who left home

Why? _____

Let a committee of children tabulate the ballots. Discuss the results (also *content; meaning-you*).

4. Use open-ended stories. Tell a Bible story, but stop before the end. "How do you think it ends?" Or, complete a story and ask, "How else might it have ended?" (also *meaning-you*).

To Discover and Express Meaning for You

Children are helped to discover that the Bible has meaning for other people when persons who are important to them willingly share these meanings. This can happen in the church school class if adults really hear what children are saying and respond to them openly and freely. Where several teachers share in leadership, children can usually find at least one adult with whom they can develop this kind of relationship.

Special activities can help children discover ways that people share meanings.

1. Let the children sponsor a Bible exhibit for the entire church. Ask people who bring Bibles to prepare a short statement telling why this particular Bible is important to them. Display the statement near the Bible. Label each Bible with the name of the owner, name of Bible edition, and date. Help children arrange the Bibles according to the reasons for their importance to the owners (also *meaning-me; backgrounds*).

2. Guide children in a study of art masterpieces that depict Bible stories. "How do you think the artist wants us to feel about the people in the story?" A helpful resource is Kathleen Sladen's book, *Are You in the Picture?* (also *content; meaning-me, -them*).

To Discover and Express Meaning for Them

"I wonder what this song from the Bible meant to the first people who ever sang it?"

"I wonder what the people in the church at Corinth thought when they got Paul's first letter?"

Because children are in a group situation when these questions are posed, the "wondering" mood can escalate as one child's thoughts spark the imaginations of others. With early elementary and younger children perhaps it is enough just to raise the wonder question frequently.

Older elementary children, with their growing sense of history, can begin to engage in the kind of research activities that will take them back and into the feelings and thoughts of those who first heard and wrote the Bible narratives.

1. Try a class project in two parts. First, make a "documentary" of a Bible event using slides, film, video tape, or black-and-white photos. Write an accompanying script in terse, journalistic style. Second, write editorials to interpret the event. Share both documentary and editorials with another group of children or at a church family night (also *meaning-me; backgrounds; skills*).

2. Present a Bible story—for example, Moses returning from the mountaintop after receiving the Ten Commandments, Paul's sermon in Athens, the feeding of the five thousand, the crucifixion, or the money changers in the temple. Rather than concentrating on the main characters, as is usually done, lead the children in dramatizing the feelings and reactions of those unnamed persons who witnessed these events (also *meaning-me*).

To Discover and Express Meaning for Us

In group/team teaching the class becomes a visible Christian community and therefore a proper place in which Bible meanings for the church today can be discovered. Teachers who use the suggested lesson plan on the "Lost Sheep" (page 123) might be tempted to maneuver the conversation until the children declared, "It means that we ought to bring more children to Sunday school next Sunday." This answer, if freely given and consciously agreed upon by the group, can be the "meaning for us in our Christian community." The answer as a result of manipulation, however, means nothing.

In addition to what it means for the class itself to be "the church," activities can help children feel a part of the larger church community.

1. Even younger children will sense the importance of the Bible to the total Christian community if they visit the sanctuary and see the Bible there. Conversation might include: Who gave it to the church? Who uses it? How is it like other Bibles? Activities while in the sanctuary could include hearing a favorite Bible story read (also *content; meaning-you*).

2. Tell a Bible story while children are looking at a stained glass window that tells the same story. Wonder together about this question: Why did people want this story in the window of this church? Plan to interview someone who might know the answer (also *content; meaning-you*).

To Absorb Bible Backgrounds

Too much conscious emphasis on geography, climate, or customs will impede the flow of a story and detract from the experience of it. However, stories and dramatizations that are effective teaching methods in the group/team teaching approach can carry along with them, quite unobtrusively, much of the background materials of the Bible.

Occasionally special activities can be planned:

1. Show the filmstrip, "A Gift from the Past" (35 mm, 70 frames, 33⅓ rpm record, guide and script, color, Graded Press). After viewing it, let the children help make *slurry*. This is a parchmentlike substance similar to paper on which early writings were recorded. The recipe is on frames 29-34 of the filmstrip (also *meaning-you*).

2. Pose living Bible pictures. Provide pictures of Bible stories or scenes of village life in Bible times. Collect materials needed for props. Let the children choose the picture they would like to pose. Take pictures with a Polaroid camera and post them beside the Bible picture (also *content*).

To Acquire Bible Skills

Basic Bible reference skills can be taught to a large group in less time than it would take to instruct each child individually. When children first receive their Bibles they will be eager to learn how to use them. As a group they can be led through the familiar steps: (1) "Find the middle of the book. This is Psalms. It is in the Old Testament." (2) "Start at the back of the Bible and go forward until you find Matthew. This is the beginning of the New Testament." And so on.

Once these elementary skills are learned it is unlikely that an entire group will again have equal reference skills or the same level of interest in their use. However, where there is a team of teachers it is possible for children to work in a separate Bible skill group with one of the team members from time to time. This interest can be stimulated by a total group activity.

1. Narrate an event recorded in the Bible. Provide an outline map with asterisks to indicate the places mentioned in the story. Instead of place names, substitute Bible references. When children find the right Bible verse they can record the place named in it beside the appropriate asterisk.

2. Teach a hymn based on a Bible text. Challenge some of the children to compare the hymn with the biblical source. Some hymns that might be used are:

    "All Things Bright and Beautiful" ......Genesis 1
    "The Lord's My Shepherd, I'll Not Want" Psalm 23
    "Joy to the World" ....Psalm 98
    "All People that on Earth Do Dwell" ...Psalm 100
    "Hosanna, Loud Hosanna" ....Matthew 21:1-12
    "While Shepherds Watched Their Flocks"
    ....Luke 2:8-14
    "Away in a Manger" ....Luke 2:15-20
    Watch for songs based on Bible texts that are included with the children's curriculum materials.

The group/team teaching approach is an excellent model for teaching the Bible. The numerous opportunities for interaction and sharing that this approach provides help children experience Bible content and discover Bible meanings. One problem is that reference skills usually develop best on an individual basis. A danger in the group/team approach is that through oversight and because of many activities the characteristics and needs of individual children may be overlooked.

Many of the curriculum materials now used by churches are based on the group/team concept. Most of the teaching suggestions there will be helpful, especially if they are used in relation to the key words: Experience! Discover and express (for me—you—them—us)! Absorb! Acquire!

2.
Discovery in Learning Centers

For more than a generation, group/team teaching has served the church school well. But "new occasions teach new duties," and "time makes ancient good uncouth." Changing styles in public school teaching, waning attendance in church schools, general restlessness and desire for change, commitment on the part of Christian educators to seek new and better approaches—all have led to an era of creativity and healthy experimentation. The learning center in the church is one of the results of this new mood.

A Learning Center Is ...

There are three visible characteristics that identify a learning center: first, the room set-up itself; second, the mobility of the students; and third, the behavior of the adults who in traditional settings are known as teachers.

The Room Set-up

Most noticeable is the absence of rows of chairs. A visitor might ask, "But where is the front of the room?" The answer, "In a room with a 'front' it is easy for the teacher to become the center around which learning is organized. In a learning center the orientation is around children and their participation in many different centers of activity."

Certain basic centers are almost always present.

The *Music Center* includes the piano, record players, rhythm instruments, song charts, and perhaps an autoharp or chimes.

The *Audio-Visual Center* provides a place to view projected pictures and includes record players, tape cassettes, and projectors. Tapes for listening may be found here or in a special *Tape Center*. Headsets for individual listening are both fun and convenient, but not essential.

The *Paint Center* is a favorite spot for many children, providing an opportunity for expression and creativity. Fingerpaints, poster paints, and water colors are all found there.

Another *Art Center*, this time for dry art, is the place to use paste, scissors, crayons, and chalk. This is the base for making such things as collages, mobiles, string art, posters, and banners.

The *Book Center* contains Bibles in several different versions and appropriate books for each age level. In addition to a display table or bookshelf, a large rug and big pillows or old sofa cushions make it an inviting and comfortable spot.

The number of other centers provided is limited only by the limits of ingenuity, space, or available leadership.

A *Drama Center* contains a prop box, puppets, ideas for creative drama, and plays for reading or pantomiming.

A *Story Center* is presided over by a good storyteller. This is of special value for younger and early elementary children or other limited readers.

Another center may include games, riddles, circuit boards, "surprise packages," or wonders of nature, and will be named according to its primary purpose—*Nature Center, Science Center, Game Center,* or perhaps the more general designation, *Discovery Center.*

For children who simply need to visit with one another for a while, a *Conversation Center* limited to two children at a time can provide a quiet retreat.

Still other centers might feature cooking or large construction activities. Centers are scattered about the room according to the placement of electrical outlets, sources of water, space, traffic flow requirements, the degree of isolation required, and the desire to achieve the feeling that "we are one big learning community." (See learning center floor plan.)

The Children

Confidence that children can initiate their own learning is one of the characteristics of a learning center. Children have a free choice of activities because, regardless of the center chosen, learning can take place. As children become involved in activities, they are allowed to work at their own speed and at their own level of ability. They can move about the room as needed, and when help is required they seek it from adults and children alike. Finally, their ability to initiate their own learning is evident even as they conclude one activity and choose another.

The Teachers/Facilitators/Enablers

A learning center requires several adults who are familiar with the center and who share responsibility for the session. In this sense it is like team teaching. In learning centers, however, the team is not working together to move children as a group from one activity to another during the session. Rather, each team member seeks to help individual children move through the session according to each child's own pattern of interests and abilities, enabling children to discover their own meanings as they explore the activities they themselves have chosen.

A CHURCH LEARNING CENTER

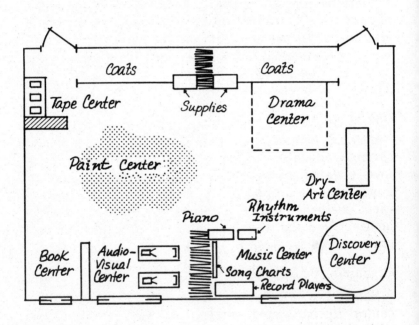

Based on the Learning Center at First United Methodist Church, Evanston, Illinois.

The adults working in the learning center might be called teachers or facilitators or enablers. They do not solve children's problems, but help children find solutions; they do not nag, but encourage; they do not hover over children, but they make themselves available. When possible, they participate in the activities along with the children.

But Learning Centers Differ

Every learning center has its own personality. In spite of similarities, there are many minor differences and at least three major ones:
>—the age of the participants
>—the organizing principle
>—the choice and duration of activities.

Age Groupings

Learning centers can be planned for a single age group, several grade levels, or for a broad age range. Churches in Iowa have experimented with learning centers for first grade through junior high school.[1] Other churches have tried intergenerational learning centers. More typical, however, are the programs planned for children from grades one through six.

Organizing Principle

Sometimes learning centers are organized around a central theme. This theme can be based on the Bible,

---

[1] *Kaleid-a-quest*, "Being A Christian Today." Warren Webb, coordinator, produced by Cedar Rapids [Iowa] District Christian Education Workshop, United Methodist Church, 1974.

church history, theology, or current issues. Whatever the theme, the activities should provide a variety of things to learn. Some activities help children discover facts; some help them discover ideas; some activities help them express and share with others the meaning of these facts and concepts.

At other times, the purpose of the learning center is to create an environment in which *interpersonal relationships* can take place. Here what is learned is not expressed in information and ideas, but in the emotional, social, and religious growth that takes place. The nature of the activity itself is not as important as the opportunity it presents for children to relate to one another in meaningful ways.

Some learning centers have as their primary goal the development of the *individual child*. Raw materials for discovery, creativity, and expression are available in each center, and children are encouraged to experiment with the materials in any way that is satisfying to them. The Music Center might contain pieces of wood, water glasses, spoons, and oatmeal boxes with which children could make music. The Art Center would have crayons, paste, scissors, string, paper, and so on, but no directions for a specific activity. Other centers would be planned accordingly. Here the emphasis is self-identity. Adult leaders stand ready to relate to each child in whatever way will be most helpful.

The thematic approach is the obvious choice when we are interested in discovering meanings in the Bible itself. However, Bible activities can also be of value when the other organizing principles are used.

The Choice and Duration of Activities

All learning centers are based on the assumption that children have free choice of activities. How children choose from among the activities and the length of time they are expected to remain with each choice are two ways learning centers differ.

Some learning centers consist of four or five individual centers, each one supervised by an adult who is prepared to guide children in the activities there. The child's choice of a center can be influenced by the kind of activity that is planned, the adult assigned to that center, or the desire to be with other children who are making that choice. When children choose a center they are expected to remain with that group for the entire session—perhaps several sessions. This kind of a learning center is similar to some styles of group/team teaching.

Other learning centers assume that in each session children will participate in several activities. They may complete two or three different projects in the same center or move from center to center. The choice here probably depends largely on the eye appeal of the various activities.

A group of Christian educators in northern Illinois have pioneered in the development of a learning center style called "independent study." The learning center is equipped with everything that will be needed for a thirteen-session unit. Guidance does not come primarily from a teacher, but from a child's guidebook of activities based on the denomination's pupil's book.[2] How children

[2] *Auto-cycle*, written and produced by Christian educators of the Northern Illinois Conference of The United Methodist Church. Elementary I-II, III-IV, V-VI. 1971, 1972, 1973, 1974, and 1975.

choose from among these activities depends on the curiosity aroused by the writing style, the child's own interest in the subject of the activity, its perceived difficulty, and the degree of fun it can be expected to provide.

Regardless of the age grouping, the variety of activities, or the organizing principle, some children will always choose to paint!

Understandings on Which Learning Centers Build

The Bible says, "Here I am—discover me!" The opportunities for total involvement and individual decisions make the learning center model an ideal setting for learning by discovery.

The learning center concept builds on many of the things we know about children:

—Each child learns at a different rate of
  speed.
—Children of the same age have different
  levels of comprehension.
—Children can develop rules by which
  to govern themselves.
—Children are curious and motivated
  by something new.
—Elementary children are interested
  in here-and-now experiences.
—Children enjoy manipulating, making, doing,
  and seeing results.

The learning center concept builds on some of the needs of children:

—In a time of increasing knowledge, children need
  to learn to find and evaluate information
  more than they need to retain it.

—Children need to be treated as individuals.

—Children need to have one-to-one relationships with persons important to them.

—Children need the opportunity to express their feelings.

—Children need the opportunity to develop a sense of independence.

Learning Centers and the Bible-Learning Tasks

Bible-learning tasks can be the basis for a learning-center design. Imagine that the learning center described on pages 136-37 is set up for four sessions. The unifying theme is "The Bible Tells Us About Jesus." Children in grades one through six are free to move from one center to another during the sessions. Activities that will help children in their Bible-learning tasks are described according to the center where they originate. The task toward which each activity is directed is indicated by the code on page 123.

Audio-Visual Center

1. *The Lost Coin (content; meaning-me).* A poster announces:

     —A coin is hidden in this room in plain sight. Can you find it? *Do not show it to anyone!*

     —When you find it leave it there, and come back and look at the filmstrip, *The Lost Coin.*[3]

   The script for the filmstrip is taped, and at the end of the tape is this instruction:

     —Now find the poster in the learning center titled, *The Lost Coin.* Do what it tells you to do. Or, paint

[3] *The Lost Coin*, filmstrip, Bible Books for Small People Series (Camden, N.J.: Thomas Nelson).

143

how you felt when you couldn't find the coin and then how you felt when you found it.

The instructions on the poster read:

—If God is the woman and you are the lost coin, how does God feel about you? Write your ideas here.

2. *Jesus and His Disciples* (*meaning-me; meaning-you, backgrounds*). A large manila envelope is near a filmstrip projector. On the envelope is printed:

—Ask a friend to join you. Look at the filmstrip in this envelope. Use the cassette tape in the envelope.

In the envelope is the filmstrip, *Jesus and His Disciples.*[4] The script is taped, and at the end of the tape are these directions:

—Now, each of you take a worksheet from the envelope. Work on it together, or do it alone, and then see if you get the same answers.

Worksheet for Filmstrip: Jesus and His Disciples
(The worksheet is arranged so that even the youngest children can satisfactorily complete some of the answers, while older children are challenged to struggle with the more difficult ideas in the biblical text.)
What disciple told the story on the filmstrip?

P__ __ __ __.

What was his job before he met Jesus?

f__ s h __ __ m a n

Jesus told Peter and his friends, "I will make you fishers of __ __ __."

[4] *Jesus and His Disciples,* filmstrip, Board of Christian Education and Publications, Evangelical and Reformed Church and the Division of Christian Education, Congregational Christian Churches, 1957.

Jesus said to the disciples, "Follow me." Another name
for those who follow Jesus is

d __ s c __ __ __ __ s.

The disciples were sometimes called

"f __ l l __ __ e r s of Jesus."

Did the disciples always understand what Jesus meant by
what he said? Yes No (Circle the one you think.)

What do *you* think Jesus meant when he told Peter
and his friends, "I will make you fishers of men?"
Write your ideas here.

_____

_____

_____

Drama Center

Provide two boxes to be kept in the Drama Center. One
will be a prop box, the other a box marked Try One of
These, which contains suggestions for drama activities.

1. "Jesus Visits Friends" (*meaning-us, -me, -you;
   backgrounds*). In a large manila envelope are three
   copies of a play based on the visit of Jesus to the home
   of Mary and Martha. These instructions are on the
   envelope:

   —Find two friends. Read and act out the play found
   in this envelope. Then talk to people in the learning center about this question: "If Jesus came to
   visit us in our church today, what should we talk
   about with him?"

2. "Palm Sunday" (*content; backgrounds*). An envelope
   contains a cassette tape. On the envelope are printed
   these instructions:

   —Ask three or four friends to listen to this tape with

145

you. Then see if you can do what it tells you to do. On the tape is recorded one of the Bible stories of Jesus' entry into Jerusalem. At the conclusion the voice on the tape suggests that the children act out the story without using words because the tape will provide the narration. The story is then recorded again, this time with long pauses between each piece of action.

3. "Holy Week"[5] (meaning-me, -them; backgrounds; skills). An envelope contains a blank tape. On the envelope are these instructions:
   —Prepare a newscast about the last week of Jesus' life as if you were there. Ask someone to help if you wish. Record it on this tape. Share it during the closing "Together Time."

Paint/Art Center

In order to leave the table free for painting, activity cards are made into a mobile and hung low over the paint table so that children can easily read the instructions.

1. Paint a picture of your favorite place. Then paint a picture of one of Jesus' favorite places. Look in the Book Center for ideas (backgrounds).
2. Hum a song you know about Jesus. Then paint how it makes you feel. Go to the Music Center for ideas (meaning-me).
3. On a small table are materials for collage-making and a sign that reads:

---

[5] Northern Illinois [United Methodist] Auto-cycle Committee, *Auto-cycle, Elementary V-VI,* ed. Gayle George (Northern Illinois United Methodist Church Conference, 1974). Adapted and used by permission.

—Tell about the resurrection of Jesus. Use anything on this table (meaning-me).

4. Draw a picture of someone that you don't like. Then go to the Audio-Visual Center and listen to the tape marked Jesus and Zaccheus (content; meaning-me; backgrounds).

On the tape is recorded the story, either directly from the Bible or from a Bible-story book.[6] At the end of the tape are recorded these instructions:

—Now go back to the Paint Center and paint a picture showing something good you can do for that person you don't like.

The Story Center

Beside the storyteller is a sign with these words:

Choose a Story

1. "The Man Who Couldn't Walk"
2. "Five Thousand Hungry People"
3. "Serious Questions"

The storyteller responds to the child's choices in these ways:

1. "Jesus and the Lame Man" (backgrounds; content). The storyteller reads the story exactly as written in Matthew 9:1-18. When finished the storyteller says:
    Now go and tell the story to a friend in the learning center, and then both of you come back to see me.

---

[6] For example, Betty Ellingboe, The Little Man from Jericho (Minneapolis: Augsburg Publishing House, 1963).

When they return the friend repeats the story for the storyteller. The storyteller reads the story from the Bible again, and together all three talk about how the story changed in retelling it only twice. This provides a chance to introduce the concept of the oral tradition.

2. "Jesus Feeds Five Thousand People" (*meaning-them; content; meaning-me; backgrounds*). The storyteller relates the story and then asks the children this question:

How do you think the people in the story felt about Jesus?

3. "Jesus Asks Serious Questions" (*meaning-me; content; backgrounds*). The story is told of Jesus' visit to the temple when he was twelve years old, especially his conversation with the temple teachers. Children are then directed to a poster titled:

Our Big Questions

What big, important questions do you have? Write them here.

Music Center

1. Songs about Jesus are mounted on pieces of cardboard and marked for use with chimes or autoharp (*content*).
2. "Hidden Treasure" (*meaning-me; content; skills*). On the wall is a poster with this heading and these instructions:

Hidden Treasure

Listen to the record, "He Bought the Whole Field." [7]

Find the same story in the Bible (Matthew 13:44).

[7] Record in packet, Elementary III-IV, Graded Press (Winter 1974).

Listen to the record again.

Tell someone in the learning center something that is so important to you that you would give almost anything for it.

3. Another poster reads:

Find a friend to help you. Read Psalm 150. While one reads it out loud, let the other praise God with rhythm instruments. Take turns (content; meaning-me).

Bible Research Center

This center is near or part of the Book Center. Envelopes containing instruction cards and duplicate materials needed are marked from 1 through 6. On the wall is a large spinner similar to those that come in boxed table games. It, too, is numbered from 1 to 6. Each child chooses an activity envelope by whirling the spinner. This center is planned primarily for the ability level of older elementary children.

1. "Gospel Parallels"[8] (skills; meaning-me).

—Find a book of Gospel parallels.[9]

Compare Mark 12:28-34; Luke 10:25-28; Matthew 22:34-40.

How many differences can you find?

Compare answers with a friend.

2. "Who Are You?" (skills; meaning-me).

—Fill in the missing words.

[8] *Auto-cycle*, Elementary V-VI.

[9] For example, *Gospel Parallels: A Synopsis of the First Three Gospels*, ed. Burton H. Throckmorton, Jr., 3rd ed. (Camden, N.J.: Thomas Nelson, 1967).

"You are the _ _ _ _ of the earth."
"You are the _ _ _ _ _ of the world."
If you need a clue, look in the Bible (Matthew 5:13,14).

3. "The Rich Young Man" (backgrounds; skills).
   —Find two friends to help you.
   Get three different versions of the Bible from the Book Center: the New English Bible, the King James Version, the Revised Standard Version. Find Mark 10:17-22 in each Bible. Read out loud to one another. Which did you like best?

4. "Revision According to You" (meaning-me, -you; skills).
   —Write Matthew 5:9 in your own words. Ask one of the adult helpers in the learning center to do it, too. Then share your ideas with one another.

5. "A Bible Hunt" (skills).
   —Find the Lord's Prayer in the Bible without being told the book, chapter, or verse.
   First, locate a concordance in the Book Center.[10] It is something like a dictionary. Look up in it the most unusual word in the first verse of the Lord's Prayer: "Our Father, who art in heaven, hallowed be thy name."
   The second part is hard! When you find the word in the concordance, ask someone to help you.

6. "Use a Bible Map" (skills).
   —If you lived in Jerusalem, which of these should

[10] For example, the concordance in the Reference Edition of the Revised Standard Version of the Bible (Camden, N.J.: Thomas Nelson, 1959), or the Concise Concordance to the Revised Standard Version of The Holy Bible (Camden, N.J.: Thomas Nelson, 1959.)

you say? "Let's go *up* to Jericho," or "Let's go
down to Jericho."
Check your answer. Find the town on a relief map
in a Bible *atlas.* [11]

Discovery Center

1. "Make a Sentence" (*skills*). In a small box are 3" X 5"
   cards on which have been written John 3:16, one word
   to a card. On the outside of the box are these instructions:
   —Arrange the words in this box into a sentence, and
     you will receive one of the most important mes-
     sages in the Bible. Clues:
     1. The first word is capitalized.
     2. The last word has a period.
     3. The second word is "God."
     4. The twelfth word has a comma.
     5. The twentieth word is "perish."
   Check your answer. Find John 3:16 in the Bible.
2. "Circuit Board" (*review*). In this center is a circuit
   board and a folder containing question/answer sheets.
   When the correct answer is chosen the board light
   goes on. Question/answer sheets contain scrambled
   versions of the following pairs:

   People Jesus Knew

   He climbed a tree ....Zaccheus
   He baptized Jesus ....John the Baptist
   She visited with Jesus ....Mary
   She was too busy to talk with Jesus ......Martha
   He used to be a fisherman ....Peter

[11] For example, *Westminster Historical Atlas to the Bible*, ed. George Ernest
Wright and Floyd Vivian Filson (Philadelphia: The Westminster Press, 1956.)

Places Jesus Knew

Jesus asked some serious questions . . .the temple
Jesus visits Mary and Martha . . . . .Bethany
A man is helped by a good
Samaritan . . . . .the Jericho Road
Where Jesus found some of his
disciples . . . . .the seashore
Where the prodigal son went . . . . .the city

3. "Treasure Hunt" [12] (backgrounds). A very small Bible has been placed in a small envelope. It has been inserted into larger envelopes, one at a time, until there are five envelopes in all. Envelopes have been numbered 1 through 5, beginning with the outside envelope. On the envelopes have been written the following clues:

   1. Can you guess what I am? See if you are right. Take me out of the envelope.
   2. I am something you can use.
   3. Many people helped create me.
   4. I contain history, laws, and letters.
   5. I tell you stories about Jesus.

4. "Grab Bag" [13] (meaning-them, -you; skills). A large bag labeled Look Inside contains a loaf of bread, a light bulb, and a vine with a small branch (or pictures of them). Also in the bag is an instruction card:

   Are these strange things to find at church?
   Read John 6:35, 8:12, and 15:5.
   What was the writer of John telling us about Jesus?

[12] Auto-cycle, Elementary V-VI.
[13] Ibid.

Problems and Possibilities

The learning center approach has great value as a teaching-learning model, but in terms of childhood's Bible-learning tasks it also has some serious problems. Because of its potential, it is important to find ways to reinforce it at its three major points of weakness: a community that appears to be fragmented, a limited amount of interaction between children and children and between children and teachers, and the possibility that the Bible may never be experienced as an Event.

Problems

One of the ways children learn what it means to be a Christian is by living among Christians in a loving and caring relationship. In some ways a learning center is a fragmented experience. The individual nature of many learning center activities prevents that visible gathering together of people that we have come to associate with Christian community. To be sure, there is a sense in which individuals at work on separate tasks can feel fellowship with one another, especially if they are aware of common goals and loyalties. Whether or not children are aware of this oneness is, of course, the question. A feeling of separation is less likely to occur when children remain in a center for at least a full session.

One hazard is that children can have thought-provoking experiences but not have interaction with others about these experiences. Instruction cards or tapes can urge children to explore their own thoughts by asking, "What does this story mean to you?" Those same cards and tapes can suggest ways to express this meaning by directing the child to another activity: "Paint how it makes you feel," or "Write beside the picture what you think the story means," or even "Tell someone in the learning center about the story." But there is no guarantee that these actions will lead to genuine dialogue.

Another question posed by the learning center model is the extent to which it can help children really experience the Bible, rather than merely learn its content. A challenge for any approach, it is most difficult when an activity is essentially an individual one. Reading a Bible story alone or watching it on a screen in isolation rarely produces the same degree of intensity as that created by a good storyteller and an attentive audience.

Possibilities

Fortunately, there are ways to overcome the problems of the learning-center model.

A good storyteller is a must! A well-told story is one of the best ways to help children experience the Bible. For a few moments they are taken out of their world into the world of Abraham, Amos, Dorcas, or Paul. When they return to their world, something of Abraham, Amos, Dorcas, and Paul returns with them. In addition, when the story has come to an end the storyteller is there, ready to respond to the spontaneous comments of the children.

But how can a storyteller be a part of a learning center? Let the storyteller preside over an attractive, cozy Story Center. The storyteller can wear a cobbler apron, a smock, or a work coat that has had many pockets added, both inside and out. Each pocket can contain gadgets, pictures, puppets—anything that will help tell the story hidden in that pocket. Children can choose a story by choosing either a pocket or a story title.

How will children know it is story time? A "gate" to the Story Center can be made. When it is open children can come. When it is closed, storytelling is in session and children must wait until later. Or, when a storyteller is ready for a new group a sound signal may be given with a triangle or chimes. Each session will have several story opportunities.

The storyteller can bring life to the Bible text and can replace solitary introspection with conversation.

A sharing-together time is a must! When everyone comes together at the close of the session for a brief time of sharing—no more than ten minutes—the learning community becomes visible. Moreover, children and adults have a chance to share what they have experienced. A first grader in one learning center wanted to read a prayer she had written. The leader suggested that this be their prayer for the morning. With all heads bowed the first grader read, "Dear God, thank you for my dolls. Amen." There were no snickers or amused glances. Her contribution had been accepted as an important part of the community's celebration of its life together.

Sensitive and alert adult leaders are a must! An attitude of openness to questions, acceptance of ideas, and willingness to share one's own understandings will encourage children to seek out adult responses. The best way for adult leaders to make themselves available is to participate in the activities of the learning center as much as possible. Adults who join children as they fingerpaint how the lost sheep must have felt have taken a giant stride toward significant interaction with children. Instead of "How did the sheep feel when it was lost?" the conversation can include, "See my picture? Sometimes I feel lost, too."

The strength of the learning-center approach is that it takes into account the need for children to be allowed to explore, discover, learn, and grow at their own speed and according to their own interests and abilities.

The weaknesses can be compensated for by the presence of a good storyteller, by sensitive and alert teachers, and by an opportunity in the closing moments of the session to share meanings and experience the joy of Christian community.

By building on the strong points and reinforcing the weak ones, the learning center provides an exciting setting in which children can begin to achieve childhood's Bible-learning tasks.

3.
Discovery in
Intergenerational Groups

Until the beginning of this century almost all religious education included everybody from children to older adults; it was intergenerational, not because it was seen to have special value, but because the church had not yet taken into account the nature of childhood. Today there is a growing conviction that some kinds of learning can take place because of the wide age range, not in spite of it.

Intergenerational Learning Is . . .

Only one characteristic distinguishes it from all other teaching-learning models—it is "intentionally intergenerational."

Variety of Goals and Groupings

One of the early reasons for interest in intergenerational activities was the need for family solidarity. The "generation gap," the "dispersed family," and a deterioration of traditional family structures were all felt to be related. "The family that plays together, stays together" became the rallying cry for family fun nights at the church.

It soon became apparent, however, that something more than fun was needed. Families needed to share in guided group activities that would provide opportunities to experience together and to think together about the meaning of that experience. Pioneered by Dr. Margaret Sawin, the Family Cluster Plan has been developed to meet this kind of need. Its intention is to prevent family crises, not to provide therapy. Skilled leadership is an essential for this model. Since lasting improvement in the quality of life together is seen as one of the primary goals of religious education, it is appropriate for these groups to discuss themes such as "Power in the Family," "Death," "Sexuality," "Conflict Resolution," "Problem-Solving," and "Beliefs and Values."

Not all intergenerational groups are interested in this pre-crisis kind of family grouping. In fact, some want to establish a pattern that is intergenerational but not always family-centered, feeling that it is good for people to relate across generational lines without being bound by established family expectations. In this design "singles," are legitimate members of such groups. The emphasis is not on the development of family life, but tends more toward themes in the areas of Bible, church history, or contemporary social issues, for example.

Often intergenerational activities are planned for children, youth, and adults. Sometimes activities include only children and adults or only youth and adults. But even three generations of adults is intergenerational.

Variety of Teaching Methods

Saying "intergenerational" says nothing about methods of teaching. The essential in choosing methods is to be sure they promote communication between the generations.

Most intergenerational groups use some variation of the group/team teaching approach. There is a theme, and certain people are designated to be leaders. The theme is introduced in some way to the total group. A small group activity follows, often in family clusters and usually experiential in nature. After each group shares with the total group, the session closes with worship.

Some churches that have had success with learning centers for children are beginning to experiment with learning centers that are intergenerational. This is an innovation that provides unique possibilities.

Values and Guidelines

In an intergenerational setting, children associate with adults other than parents and teachers. They enter into thoughtful discussions when these discussions are at their level and often are challenged to stretch their minds. They hear differences of opinion and learn to sort and choose. And hopefully, they experience the stability of belonging to a Christian community in the midst of a changing world.

Not only the young benefit from intergenerational learning. When adults seriously participate in dialogue across the ages, they find that they can no longer mask their theological questions behind abstract words. Nor, in the presence of children who are tuned to the present can they separate the Bible they read from the life they live. The willingness of children to express themselves in fingerpainting or clapping to music releases adults to express feelings and ideas in ways other than words.

The intergenerational nature of the setting means that children, perhaps for the first time, are considered an important and equal part of what looks like an adult gathering and that adults, perhaps for the first time, are considered something other than in charge of what looks like a children's group. It is not like a Thanksgiving family reunion when women cook, men talk, and children play; or like Christmas, when adults give and children receive; or like some church worship services, where adults listen and children squirm. Instead, everyone gives and everyone receives. The presence of this kind of dialogue is one of the criteria by which success is measured.

To achieve a successful intergenerational group, three guidelines are offered:

When plans are made, persons of every age ought to be seen as equal in importance. There are no second-class citizens in the Christian church. A session is not planned for those in one age bracket, slighting the others.

Plans ought to build on what each age group has to offer. A child may pose a question that an adult is reluctant to ask or express an insight that a self-conscious adult would hold back from fear of sounding naïve. An adult may provide a piece of information, a new interpretation, or a manual skill needed by a child.

An intergenerational learning group ought to challenge the adult intellect. The difficulty of this and the failure to accomplish it are major criticisms of intergenerational study.

Bible-Learning Tasks in Intergenerational Settings

Because of the variety of age groups, goals, and methods, it is impossible to describe a typical ten-minute segment or a typical room arrangement for intergenerational groups. There are four forms of intergenerational activities that can be isolated: the Bible in the home, the church night, the weekend camp, and the study series. Each is discussed below in relation to childhood's Bible-learning tasks.

The Bible in the Home

The first intergenerational relationship is the one between the mother and the newborn child. For most children this quickly broadens to include all the other members of the family.

The Bible is taught indirectly when children see that daily life in the family is consistent with the beliefs declared publicly on Sunday. The Bible itself can consciously be used in family worship and Bible stories can sometimes be included in family story times.

The same principles of teaching the Bible that were outlined in Section III: Teaching can be used by parents as the child's first teacher of religion. For example, the conversation ideas on pages 124-25 would be as appropriate for a parent to use at home with children after reading the story of "The Lost Sheep" as they are for a team of teachers in the church school.

The Church Night

One of the earliest forms of intergenerational learning in a church setting was the occasional "church night" or

161

"family night." Too often the ride to the church in the family car was the only intergenerational aspect of the evening because families were divided into age groups as soon as they entered the church doors. Today those who intentionally seek intergenerational experiences plan a vastly different format.

The occasional church night may occur once a month, once a quarter, or perhaps only two or three times a year. Usually held in the church, it may or may not be preceded by a meal. Sometimes the event may be planned for a "Y" swimming pool, a park, or a theater.

It is reasonably easy to plan an evening of fun that is intergenerational. It is more difficult to provide an evening of Bible study that does not divide people into age groups. It was this difficulty, after all, that led to the development of group-graded curriculum materials.

A successful intergenerational study needs to provide a variety of activities, to be fast moving, and to have meaning for all ages. In addition, when a biblical theme is used, those who plan the program should keep in mind the Bible-learning tasks of content to be experienced, meaning to be discovered, backgrounds to be absorbed, and skills to be acquired.

Here is one possibility for a church-night program:

A Church-Night Outline: "Stories Around Campfires"
Room Arrangement: Around the room are group leaders dressed as nomads, one for every fifteen people expected. On the wall near each leader is posted several pictures of ancient Hebrew families. A few chairs are available at each site for those who cannot sit on the floor.

As People Arrive: They are directed to one of the small groups, where the leader encourages them to discuss the pictures—the clothes, the tent, the cooking, and the animals (backgrounds).

Summarizing: At a signal from the program leader each small group helps its leader list on a piece of newsprint the things they have noticed in the pictures (background).

Scene Setting: The program leader announces to all that:
—Everyone present is a member of an ancient Hebrew nomadic clan.
—They all need to look like nomads. (A box of cloth strips is given to each group from which men and boys immediately fashion turbans or wide waistbands, and women and girls, scarves.)
—Each clan needs a campfire. A box of wood or twigs, a flashlight, and red cellophane are given to each group from which they construct a "campfire" (background).

Daily Life Drama: While the program leader narrates, each clan pantomimes the following daily routines:
—lighting the fire
—preparing the evening meal
—caring for the animals

Campfire Circle: Lights are dimmed and each clan sits around its campfire. In each clan a child who·has been prompted asks of the clan chief (the leader of that group), "Tell us a story?" Here, any one of the early Old Testament stories is told, and when the storyteller finishes he invites responses and questions from the group (meaning-me, -you, -them).

Group Singing: All clans join to form a tribe. They combine the "campfires" to make one large one and conclude the evening with singing.

The Weekend Camp

A newer setting for intergenerational learning is the weekend camp. Usually billed as a "family camp," the church-sponsored weekend outing is becoming increasingly popular. Some of these are planned as retreats for parents where they can relax while their children are supervised by someone else. As valuable as this may be, it is not what is meant by intergenerational learning in a weekend camp setting.

In addition to the desire to study the Bible in an intentionally intergenerational setting, there are two other guidelines for those who plan for an outdoor experience. First, let the natural setting suggest some of the teaching methods, and second, let the natural setting suggest some of the Bible content.

Programs appropriate to the church building should be left there. If Bible study takes place around tables at the church, why go to camp in order to sit around tables? Try a shady spot under a tree, a beach, or even a boat. For the weekend, replace recorded music with songs of the birds, the rustle of wind in the trees, the howl of coyotes, or the rushing sound of water as it tumbles over the rocks. Leave filmstrip projectors at the church and create story lines for the panorama of nature unfolding in every direction. Instead of craft materials from hobby shops, use the sand, dirt, rocks, twigs, leaves, weeds, flowers, and pine cones from the campsite.

Camping is an ideal way to experience the life of the ancient nomads—living in tents, cooking over open fires, battling the weather, and sitting around the campfire at night, wondering together about the meaning of it all. A rest stop during a long hike and a drink of cool water from the canteens or a stream can be the occasion for telling the story of Isaac and the wells. A sudden storm over the lake might suggest the story of Jesus calming the waters, or recall the adventure of Paul and the shipwreck. The rainbow following the storm can remind campers of the Old Testament story of God's covenant with Noah.

In addition to these unplanned learning experiences, there can be planned activities that are appropriate to the setting. Here is one suggestion:

Weekend Camp Theme: "Altars"
Length of Time: One weekend

Friday Night: Unpack and set up camp.

Total Group Orientation: In addition to other necessary details, introduce the theme. Talk about altars, their purpose, and their history (*backgrounds*).

Intergenerational Activity in Small or Family Groups: Each group finds a spot within five minutes of the general meeting place. With nature materials found there they build an altar. At this point, they leave the altar bare of any symbolism (*content*).

Saturday

Morning Worship: After breakfast a good storyteller narrates the story of Esau and Jacob (Genesis 27-28:1-9) or reads it from a Bible story book (*content; meaning-them*). The small groups gather and read together the story of Jacob's altar (Genesis 28:10-22). They plan a brief worship service using as a theme,

"Surely the Lord is in this place." After deciding how group members will participate, they walk to their altar and worship.

During the Day: Members of the small groups, as they wish, make crosses or other Christian symbols for their altars (*background*).

Evening Campfire: Tell the story of Paul and Silas in prison (Acts 16:16-40), their subsequent travels and encounter with the Greeks, and Paul's sermon about the altar to "an unknown God" (Acts 17:22-28) (*content, meaning-me*).

Sunday

Total Group Worship: Theme—"Gifts and Altars." For a sermon, use portions of the Sermon on the Mount, concluding with Matthew 5:21-24 (*meaning-me, -us*).

Intergenerational Activity in Small or Family Groups: Share Christian symbols made on Saturday. Write prayers of dedication for them. Take them to the altar and arrange them. Say together the prayers of dedication (*meaning-me, -you*).

After Packing Up: Before leaving the campsite, let the final activity be the dismantling of the altars and the returning of the pieces to their natural setting. The Christian symbols can be taken home.

Study Series

There is a growing interest in intergenerational, short-term study series of varying lengths. These are in sharp contrast to the church night or weekend camp. While church nights and weekend camps are usually more concerned with fellowship than study, the intergenerational study series concentrates on study. Often held at the regular church school hour, the usual series is from four to six weeks, although some continue as long as three months. Like the learning center, the study series is often seen as a summer change of pace to the teaching style of the rest of the year.

When the intergenerational study series is held during the church school hour, it is handicapped by the limited time available—usually only one hour. However, some forms of group/team teaching or learning centers are still possible. Here is a way to combine the two:

Study Series Outline: "Stories About Jesus"

Length of Time: Six one-hour sessions.

Ages: Elementary, youth, and adults

Story Time: Fifteen minutes. The entire group experiences the same Bible story about Jesus. It may be told by an excellent storyteller, dramatized by live actors or through puppets or seen in a well-produced motion picture (content).

Learning Center: Thirty minutes. All learning-center activities relate to the story that opened the session. Activities are geared to different levels of ability. Difficulty may be indicated by a color or number code (meaning-me).

Sharing Together: Fifteen minutes. Part of this closing period may be singing and other acts of worship. The major portion of the time, however, is spent in sharing the Bible meanings discovered in the learning-center activities. Adults should share their own discoveries as well as draw responses from children, but they should not monopolize the time with details and doctrinal arguments. This is a time for each person to accept and value others' contributions (*meaning-you, -us*).

Suggested Plan for One Session of the Series
(Session Theme: "The Calling of the Disciples")

Story Time: Tell the story of the calling of the disciples, using Matthew 4:18-22, 9:9, 10:1-11; Mark 1:12-20; Luke 4:14-22, 31-43; John 1:42. Or read the story from a Bible-story book. Then, with volunteers from the group to pantomime the story, retell selected portions of it. If there is time, pantomime parts of it again with a different group of actors (*content*).

Learning Center: In the activities suggested here, (1) is the easiest and could be accomplished by first grade children, although some adults might enjoy it too. Number (9) is the most difficult and would be chosen by research-oriented youth and adults.

1. Paint a picture of Jesus calling the disciples (*meaning-me*).
2. Paint a picture of something followers of Jesus do today (*meaning-me, -us*).
3. Write a poem about how one of the disciples felt when Jesus called him (*meaning-me, -them*).
4. Write a prayer that can be shared during the Together Time today (*meaning-me*).
5. Make shields or banners of the disciples, using a book on Christian symbolism as a guide[1] (*meaning-me; backgrounds*).

[1] For example, Michael Daves, *Young Readers Book of Christian Symbolism* (Nashville: Abingdon Press, 1967).

6. List as many ways of earning a living as you can think of. Now cross out those that you could not choose and still be a follower of Jesus. Compare your list with others in the learning center who have chosen this activity (meaning-me, -you, -us).

7. "Does Jesus still 'call' people today?" You may want to discuss this with others at the "talk table." A small table labeled "Talk Table" has been set up with two or three chairs around it (meaning-me, -you, -us).

8. Find three other people about your own age. Discuss with them, "What would be different if we took modern-day discipleship seriously?" (meaning-me, -you).

9. Read Matthew 4:18-22, 9:9-13; Mark 1:16-20, 2:13-14, 3:13-19; Luke 5:1-11, 5:27-32; John 21:1-3. Make a list of all the disciples mentioned. How many are there? Now read all these references in a Bible commentary (meaning-me; backgrounds; skills).

Sharing Together: This is the time for persons to say to one another in their own way, "The calling of the disciples by Jesus means more to me now than it did forty-five minutes ago. What does it mean to you now? What can it mean for us as Christians together?" (meaning-you, -us).

Intergenerational learning is strong when vital communication across age lines occurs. Such learning is one of the best possible ways for children to discover that people find meaning in the Bible although they may find it in different ways, and that people can continue to find new meanings as they grow. This kind of learning can occur both at home and in church-planned study.

The crucial question about intergenerational study is this: Is it possible to provide a challenge for adults and children at the same time? The tendency to sacrifice adults for the sake of children is responsible for the fact that most intergenerational programs have been occasional events such as the weekend camp or church night. Nevertheless, occasional and short-term intergenerational experiences are worthy alternatives for more traditional ways of teaching the Bible.

AND SO, FORTH!

Now this particular exploration is at an end. The way the Bible can be interpreted, the nature of children, philosophies of education, and the implications of all this for helping children discover Bible meanings have been explored.

Ways in which Bible-learning tasks can be achieved have been described in terms of three models: group/team teaching, learning centers, and intergenerational groups.

For readers who have not agreed with the writer's point of view, here is a challenge to continue your own exploration, build on options you choose, and develop your own goals and models for teaching children the Bible.

For readers who have agreed, here is a challenge to experiment with one of the models described or invent some new models.

In any case, God's Word is not locked up in a book, but is loose in the world. This is the witness of the Bible writers, and this is the witness of those today who experience the Bible as an Event.

And so, forth!

FOR FURTHER READING

Section One: The Bible

Anderson, Bernhard W. *The Unfolding Drama of the Bible.* New York: Association Press, Reflection Book, 1957.

Barclay, William. *Introducing the Bible.* Nashville: Abingdon Press, 1973.

Gottwald, Norman K. *A Light to the Nations.* New York: Harper & Brothers, 1959.

Interpreter's One-Volume Commentary on the Bible. Ed. Charles M. Laymon. Nashville: Abingdon Press, 1971.

Wink, Walter. *The Bible in Human Transformation.* Philadelphia: Fortress Press, 1973.

Section Two: Children

Erikson, Erik. *Childhood and Society.* 2nd ed. New York: W. W. Norton & Co., 1963.

Flavell, John H. *The Developmental Psychology of Jean Piaget.* New York: Van Nostrand Reinhold Co., 1963.

Illich, Ivan. *Deschooling Society.* New York: Harper & Row, 1971.

Maier, Henry William. *Three Theories of Child Development.* Rev. ed. New York: Harper & Row, 1970.

Mead, Margaret. *Culture and Commitment: A Study of*

the Generation Gap. Garden City, N.Y.: Doubleday & Co., 1970.

Tofler, Alvin. *Future Shock.* New York: Random House, 1970.

Section Three: Teaching

Goldman, Ronald. *Readiness for Religion: A Basis for Developmental Religious Education.* New York: The Seabury Press, 1968.

Maves, Paul B. and Maves, Mary Carolyn. *Finding Your Way Through the Bible.* Nashville: Graded Press, 1968-1970.

Rood, Wayne. *On Nurturing Christians.* Nashville: Abingdon Press, 1972.

Section Four: Models

Young Readers Dictionary of the Bible. Nashville: Abingdon Press, 1969.

Daves, Michael. *Young Readers Book of Christian Symbolism.* Nashville: Abingdon Press, 1967.

Doss, Helen. *Young Readers Book of Bible Stories.* Nashville: Abingdon Press, 1970.

Dotts, M. Franklin and Dotts, Maryann J. *Clues to Creativity: Providing Learning Experiences for Children.* (3 vols.) New York: Friendship Press, 1974 and 1975.

Furnish, Dorothy Jean. *Auto-cycle: A Learning Center Approach to Christian Education for Children.* Published and distributed by First United Methodist Church, 1903 E. Euclid, Arlington Heights, Illinois. Copyright 1974 by the Auto-cycle Committee, Northern Illinois Conference of The United Methodist Church.

Sawin, Margaret M. *Educating by Family Groups: A New Model for Religious Education.* 1973. Distributed by Lead Consultants, P.O. Box 311, Pittsford, New York.

Sladen, Kathleen. *Are You in the Picture? Nashville: Abingdon Press, 1973.*

United Church Board for Homeland Ministries, Division of Christian Education. *The Learning Center Approach in Church Education.* 1971. Distributed by Lead Consultants, P.O. Box 311, Pittsford, New York.

Wright, Kathryn S. *Let the Children Paint: Art in Religious Education.* New York: The Seabury Press, 1966.